TEN FILM CLASSICS

TEN FILM CLASSICS

A Re-Viewing

Edward Murray

With illustrations

FREDERICK UNGAR PUBLISHING CO.
NEW YORK

For Monica

Copyright © 1978 by Frederick Ungar Publishing Co., Inc.
Printed in the United States ot America

Designed by Helen Roberts

Library of Congress Cataloging in Publication Data

Murray, Edward
   Ten film classics.

   Bibliography: p.
   Filmography: p.
   Includes index.
   CONTENTS: Potemkin (1925).—Citizen Kane (1941).
—The bicylce thief (1949).—Ikiru (1952). [etc.]
   1. Moving-picture plays—History and criticism.
   I. Title.
PN1995.M844   791.43′7   78-4293
   ISBN 0-8044-2650-3
   ISBN 0-8044-6535-5 pbk.

Photos courtesy of the Museum of Modern Art/Film Stills Archive

Preface

The films discussed in this book are among the greatest ever made. I have selected ten film classics—not *the* ten best films of all time (the latter a futile undertaking). Without doubt, I could easily have chosen ten other films, or even a hundred other films. Consider ten films I have *not* included: Griffith's *Birth of a Nation* (1915) and *Intolerance* (1916); Murnau's *The Last Laugh* (1924); Dreyer's *The Passion of Joan of Arc* (1928); Renoir's *Grand Illusion* (1937) and *The Rules of the Game* (1939); Rossellini's *Open City* (1945); Truffaut's *Jules and Jim* (1961); Fellini's 8½ (1963); and Bergman's *Persona* (1965). If the reader's favorite film is missing from my study, I assure him that many other favorites of mine have been omitted from consideration, too. I only had space to deal adequately with ten great films.

It is not easy to say in the abstract what makes a great film, or what constitutes a film classic. Technique is important. *Potemkin* (1925) is memorable because in it Eisenstein showed the world a new way to edit film; and it remains as exciting to watch today as it must have been for audiences who saw it for the first time over fifty years ago. Welles's *Citizen Kane* (1941) is justly famous for its deep-focus photography, complex flashbacks, and sound montages (or "lightning mixes"). And the fresh uses to which Penn adopted serio-comic structure in *Bonnie and Clyde* (1967) have had an enormous influence on other film-makers. But technique isn't everything. The content

v

of a film—its meaning—remains equally important. *Potemkin,
Citizen Kane, Bonnie and Clyde*—each of these films also has a
forceful theme. Other films—such as De Sica's *The Bicycle
Thief* (1949) and Kurosawa's *Ikiru* (1952)—are of enduring
interest even though they seem to lack technical brilliance. The
art of De Sica and Kurosawa lies in their ability to make us
forget the camera and the editing process. They immerse us in
the lives of their characters and their chosen surroundings, but
they do so without the stylistic flamboyance of Eisenstein,
Welles, and Penn.

But enough of generalization in advance of description,
analysis, and interpretation. In the main, I have concentrated
on a formalistic approach to these ten classics. By "re-viewing"
each of them, by showing not only *what* happens on the screen
but also *how* it happens, I hope to make the reader "see" the
film again with greater understanding and appreciation.
Wherever pertinent, I have also placed each film in a theoretical
and historical perspective. One can scarcely discuss *Potemkin*
without reference to Eisenstein's essays on montage, or *Citizen
Kane* without mentioning André Bazin. *The Bicycle Thief* and
Fellini's *La Strada* (1954) both need to be seen in the context of
Italian neo-realism—just as Truffaut's *The 400 Blows* (1959)
has to be viewed in relation to the *auteur* theory and the French
New Wave. No film is an island, entirely self-contained. Works
of art are created within a specific economic, social, and
political environment. A film like *Bonnie and Clyde* poses questions about the relationship between art and history, and about
morality and violence, on the screen.

By combining various critical approaches, I have tried to
give the reader an in-depth view of each film. Other approaches
are possible, however, and the last word on any of these masterpieces has yet to be said.

E. M.

Contents

1
Potemkin
1925

Sergei Eisenstein will be remembered not only as a major film-maker—his *Potemkin* has often been called "the greatest film ever made"—but also as one of the most important theorists of the cinema. Although he had provocative things to say about acting, sound, color, and film as a synthesis of all the arts and sciences, Eisenstein's most significant contribution to film study centers on his conception of montage.

The word "montage" comes from the French; it means "mounting" or "putting together." Sometimes montage is used loosely as a synonym for editing. Among Western film-makers, montage often means an impressionistic sequence of short shots intended to convey a sense of time passing. For Eisenstein, however, montage had a wholly different signification.

As an engineering student, Eisenstein had learned the definite laws governing the construction of roads, bridges, waterways, and the principles involved in the management of machinery. With rigorous analysis, he maintained, one could also discover the laws which determined all forms of art. From the beginning, the Soviet film was linked to the 1917 Revolution. "Of all the arts," Lenin once announced, "the cinema is the most important for us." He was thinking of propaganda. In the nineteenth century, Hegel formulated his triadic dialectic of thesis, antithesis, and synthesis; later Marx and Engels transformed the Hegelian logical-metaphysical-idealist approach into what has come to be called dialectical

1

materialism. Whereas Hegel saw the movement of the dialectic in history as a phenomenal expression of the movement of absolute thought, Marx and Engels argued that the dialectical movement of human thought merely reflects the dialectical process inherent in "reality," or nature and history. The development toward a perfect communist world, then, is based on a series of contradictions, followed by contradictions of contradictions, leading to ever higher stages in the dialectical process.

Eisenstein sought to apply this philosophy to film. Two shots different in kind (the "thesis" and the "antithesis") collide to establish a new concept (the "synthesis"). In his essay "A Dialectic Approach to Film Form" (1929), Eisenstein explains that the relationship between the shot and the subtitle on the one hand, and between the shot and montage on the other, represents dialectical phases: "Conflict within a *thesis* (an abstract idea)—*formulates* itself in the dialectics of the sub-title—*forms* itself spatially in the conflict within the shot—and *explodes* with increasing intensity in montage—conflict among the separate shots."[1] Eisenstein aimed for "pathos" in his dialectical form. He wanted to send the viewer into ecstasy, out of himself—out of passivity, and into action.

According to Eisenstein, there is a correspondence between montage and Japanese hieroglyphic writing. An ideogram results from the fusion of two separate hieroglyphs; for instance, the picture of a dog plus the picture of a mouth becomes "to bark." The ideogram is not the sum of two hieroglyphs but their product. By this distinction, Eisenstein intends that whereas each hieroglyph represents an object the ideogram stands for a concept—a value of another dimension. This, for Eisenstein, is montage—that is, the "combining [of] shots that are *depictive*, single in meaning, neutral in content—into *intellectual* contexts and series."[2] The shot is not an element of montage but a cell which, so to speak, divides to form an entity of another order. Montage is characterized not by a simple chain of pictorially continuous images but by "shock attraction"—or the clash of images—which produces a new idea.

Potemkin 1925

A shot from the Odessa Steps sequence of *Potemkin*. It is the most famous example of Eisenstein's montage and the most written-about sequence in film history.

The shots, or montage cells, have no value as separate entities. As Eisenstein observes in "Film Language" (1934), the more arresting individual images are in themselves, the more a film becomes a series of beautiful but disconnected snaphots.[3] Nevertheless, conflict exists within each specific cell; the same kind of conflict which can be found between shots can also be found within the single shot. In "A Dialectic Approach to Film Form," Eisenstein distinguishes ten such types of conflict: 1) graphic conflict; 2) conflict of planes; 3) conflict of volumes; 4) spatial conflict; 5) light conflict; 6) tempo conflict; 7) conflict between matter and viewpoint; 8) conflict between matter and its spatial nature; 9) conflict between an event and its temporal nature; and 10) conflict in terms of audio-visual counterpoint.[4] It is montage structure alone, however, which confers meaning on the individual shots.

In 1929, Eisenstein listed five kinds of montage (see "Methods of Montage"); in 1938, as a result of his work on *Alexander Nevsky* (1938), he added a sixth (see "Synchronization of Senses").[5] *Metric montage* depends on the *"absolute lengths"* of the film strips joined together in such a way as to resemble a musical beat. Content is less important here than the fixed, mechanical relation of the film strips to one another. A Griffith last-minute-rescue sequence would serve as an example for this type of montage (which, by the way, Eisenstein did not regard highly). *Rhythmic montage* shows concern for the content of a shot. Here, the mechanical considerations of metric montage surrender to an ordering of the film strips according to their *"actual* lengths." In the Odessa Steps sequence of *Potemkin*, Eisenstein informs us, the rhythmic drum of the soldiers' feet as they descend the steps violate all *metrical* demands, since the movement of the soldiers remains unsynchronized with the tempo of the cutting. *Tonal montage* points to the "general *tone"* of a piece. If a film sequence is described as having a shrill quality, one should look for angle shots and angular shapes, inasmuch as some kind of "graphic tonality" is at work. *Overtonal montage* can be distinguished from tonal montage "by the collective calculations of all the

4

piece's appeals." The superior film-maker seeks to present more than one emotional tone per shot; he calls upon the overtonal approach to reveal a number of feelings and ideas within a single image.

Metric, rhythmic, tonal, and overtonal are terms used to designate methods of montage. These methods can be described as montage constructions only when they are patterned into the duration of a shot and movement within the frame; similarly, tonal montage grows out of the clash between the rhythmic and tonal qualities of the work; finally, overtonal montage results from the clash between the major tone (its dominant) and the overtone. The four methods of montage work on the viewer at the affective—physiological level. *Intellectual montage*, however, is intended to make its appeal to the rational faculty in the viewer—it involves a conflict between ideas.

A re-viewing of *Potemkin* shows how very much the film-maker's theory remains relevant to an appreciation of his masterpiece.

In 1925, Eisenstein was instructed by the Soviet government to make a film about the abortive revolution of 1905—a film broad in scope. Only about forty shots of the 800 planned were to have been about the mutiny aboard the battleship *Potemkin*. However, when Eisenstein saw the Odessa Steps, he changed his plan and revised his script. Now, one mutiny would stand for the entire revolution. Although the 1905 rebellion failed, the Soviet authorities wanted Eisenstein to end the film optimistically.

The *Potemkin* was the pride of the Imperial Russian Navy. But poor food, including wormy meat, served to the sailors for months created a situation conducive to revolt. When a seaman complained about the food, an officer shot him; the officer, in turn, was shot by some crew members and tossed overboard. The captain and the other officers on the ship were also slain. Arriving at Odessa, the *Potemkin* received fuel and supplies from their comrades on shore. Other ships from the Black Sea fleet, however, did not join the *Potemkin* in mutiny.

Later, the men on board the battleship argued among themselves and finally decided to surrender the ship to Rumanian authorities. Some sailors managed to escape, but others were executed. In the film, Eisenstein concludes the action by showing the *Potemkin* sailing past the Czar's fleet— sailing victoriously out to sea—without a shot fired by either side. According to Eisenstein, although the revolt aboard the real *Potemkin*, like the 1905 revolution as a whole, was not ultimately successful, it foreshadowed the later triumph of 1917. The optimistic conclusion to the film therefore seemed justified.

Eisenstein divides the structure of *Potemkin* into five parts, each part titled and numbered, the five parts representing a chronological series of events: I. Men and Maggots; II. Drama on the Quarter-Deck; III. The Dead Man Cries for Vengeance; IV. The Odessa Steps; V. Meeting the Squadron. *Potemkin* is a perfect example of fragmentation editing. Whereas the average film contains about 600 shots—and though 800 had originally been planned for a film about the entire 1905 revolution—the structure of *Potemkin* is made up of 1,346 shots.

"Men and Maggots" opens with five shots of waves crashing symbolically over a jetty, and shots of waves flowing over rocks on a shore. Cut to an insert title: "Revolution is the only lawful, equal, effectual war. It was in Russia that this war was declared and begun." The quotation is from Lenin. Two seaman are introduced: Matyushenko and Vakulinchuk. The former says: "We, the sailors of the Potemkin, must support the revolution with our brothers, the workers." Thus, conflict is presented immediately, and in a clear-cut fashion. Eisenstein works by contrast: the arrogant faces of the officers versus the angry faces of the crew; the well-cut uniforms of the officers versus the plain-looking garb of the crew; the authority of the officers versus the rebelliousness of the crew. As Vakulinchuk puts it: "What are we waiting for? All Russia is rising. Are we to be the last?"

The struggle commences when the men refuse to eat any more rotten food. Smirnov, the ship's doctor, appears and examines a carcass of meat. He folds his pince-nez in half to form a magnifying lens, and informs the men that there are no maggots in the meat, though the camera-eye shows them clearly in close-up.

Like most of the performers in *Potemkin*, Smirnov is played by a nonprofessional. During the twenties, Eisenstein's films were cast on the basis of what he called "typage" theory—or what Hollywood refers to as "type casting." Whether he used professional or nonprofessional actors, Eisenstein chose them on the basis of how they looked. They were thought of as simply plastic material to be shaped by montage. Eisenstein observed the general characteristics of doctors, formed a composite image of one, and then looked for the "type." Smirnov was played by a man who knew nothing of medicine; he was, in fact, a porter. The pince-nez became identified with the doctor. Later in the film, when Smirnov is tossed overboard, his eyeglasses get caught on one of the ship's cables. Eisenstein presents the pince-nez in a close-up, thus reminding us of the earlier scene, in addition to letting the part (the glasses) stand for the whole (Smirnov himself).

Although there is a confrontation between the crew and some officers in the first part of *Potemkin*, there is no bloodshed. "Men and Maggots" ends in the ship's galley. Sailors are washing and drying the officers' plates and setting the table for dinner. One sailor reads the inscription on a plate: "Give us this day our daily bread." Slowly, his anger rises. With great force, he smashes the plate and upsets the table prepared for the officers. This symbolic action is extremely important structurally and thematically. As a result, Eisenstein prolongs its impact visually on the screen. Normally, the breaking of a dish would take about two seconds. Instead of recording the action in real time with a single shot, Eisenstein substitutes filmic time by editing nine shots from various angles in an overlapping progression, so that the breaking of the dish takes longer than it realistically would have aboard the actual *Potemkin*. The technique marks the difference between life and art.

In Part Two: "Drama on the Quarter-Deck," the officers

and crew of the *Potemkin* reach a turning point in their relationship. A bugle sounds, calling all hands to the quarter-deck. Commander Golikov roars: "All those satisfied with the food step two paces forward!" Throughout this scene, Eisenstein repeatedly shoots the action from a position in back of the two cannons which protrude threateningly over the men. The cannons symbolize the power of the government against which the men are revolting. Most of the sailors refuse to step forward. Furious, Golikov shouts: "Hang them from the yardarm!" Eisenstein cuts nervously back and forth between the men and the officers. An old sailor looks up at the yardarm. Here Eisenstein uses a subjective camera: the viewer sees what the old sailor imagines—six bodies swinging from the yardarm.

"Call out the marine guard!" cries Golikov. Just then, Matyushenko breaks rank and urges his comrades to join him at the gun-turret. The guard appears. "Now," shouts Matyushenko. "The time has come!" The majority of the sailors join him at the turret. With most of the men crowded on either side of the cannons, and with Golikov standing in the line of the cannons, Eisenstein visually suggests that the balance of power has begun to shift in favor of the men. Suspense remains, though, because we do not know how the marines will respond to Golikov's commands.

To the men who have not been able to escape from the prow of the *Potemkin*, Golikov warns: "I'll shoot you down like dogs . . . Cover them with a tarpaulin!" The order is carried out. An officer shouts: "Attention!," and the marine guard stiffens. Shot of a priest, standing with a cross raised before him: "Lord, show thyself to these unruly sinners." The sailors who are about to be shot wait in fear. "At the tarpaulin—" comes the command—"Fire!" But the marines hesitate to kill their fellow seamen. Close-up of the cross in the priest's hands; cut to a close-up of an officer's hand stroking the hilt of his dagger. The transition from one object to another, both of them shaped in a similar fashion, underlines the link between church and military in the Czarist regime.

8

Potemkin 1925

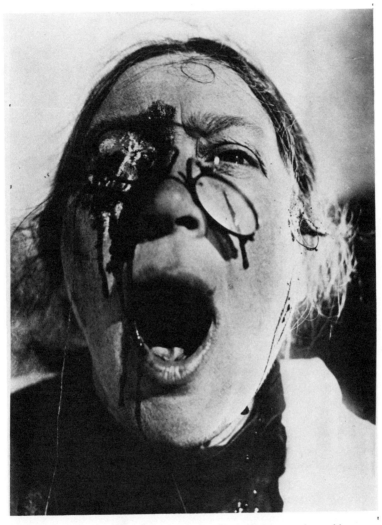

Close-up from the Odessa Steps sequence. A Cossack has struck an old woman wearing pince-nez in the right eye with his sword. We do not actually see the blow. Through "shock attraction," Eisenstein takes shots of the Cossack and a shot of the woman—shots which in themselves are "single in meaning"—and combines them to form a new concept: the woman has been slashed by the Cossack.

9

From the first command given to the marines to fire, through their agony of indecision and the torment of the intended victims, to the moment when Vakulinchuk's cry: "Brothers!" finally wins over the guard, Eisenstein edits dozens of shots together in order to sustain the tension. When it becomes clear that the guard will not kill the unhappy men, violence at last breaks out—and the tension is broken. In the battle the officers are overpowered, many of them slain, but Vakulinchuk is also killed.

Part Two ends with Vakulinchuk's body lying on the pier of Odessa, his clasped hands holding a lighted candle on his chest. A sign rests on his body: "For a spoonful of soup."

Part Three: "The Dead Man Cries for Vengeance" remains a relatively calm sequence, a bridge between the violence of both "Drama on the Quarter-Deck" and Part Four: "The Odessa Steps." At the heart of the third section is the mourning of the masses for Vakulinchuk; the mood, however, develops gradually from sorrow through anger to end on a happy, confident note. In time, the sequence moves from night to dawn.

"The Dead Man Cries for Vengeance" begins with an iris shot of Odessa as viewed from the sea. By opening with a technique which shows an image in only one small round area of the scene, Eisenstein "poetizes" his material; it is a signal that symbolism here will be more important than a documentary-like realism. Throughout *Potemkin*, Eisenstein combines realism (the film was shot on location, there are mostly non-professionals in the cast, much of the action is factual) with stylization (the extreme form of montage, with its fragmented editing, the expansion of time, and the showing of the same event more than once, such as in the Odessa Steps sequence). Tonal montage is apparent in Part Three as Eisenstein's shots are selected, initially, for their "mistiness," and later for their "brightness." In tempo, Eisenstein edits slowly at first, then builds to a brisker pace.

To symbolize the growing power of the masses' sentiments, Eisenstein shows more and more people filing past

Vakulinchuk's body. Shot of rising steps empty of people (the right and left sides of the screen are blacked out). Dissolve to a shot of the steps crowded with people. Shot of the masses ascending stairs at the edge of the pier to view the dead hero's body; behind them can be seen a narrow jetty, filled with people, stretching beyond the frame of the picture. High-angle shot of a crowd surrounding Vakulinchuk's corpse. Slow pan from the masses—to the waters of the harbor. Nothing, Eisenstein suggests, can stop the advance of the workers. Waves of people move relentlessly across the curving stairways on either side of an enormous bridge. Almost everyone in Odessa seems to support the mutineers aboard the *Potemkin*.

Almost everyone . . . Speeches are made over Vakulinchuk's body. A sailor cries: "We will avenge ourselves! Death to the oppressors!" Three women sing out: "All for one . . . one for all!" Men and women continue to harangue the crowd. But one well-dressed man persists in cynically sneering at the impassioned speakers. "Down with the Jews!" he says. Close-up of a sailor's angry face. Shots of peasants and workers glaring at the well-dressed defender of the government. Suddenly the crowd attacks the man, beating him with their fists, driving him to the ground. "Shoulder to shoulder!" screams an agitator. Shot of men and women moving down two large stairways, advancing under the arch of a bridge. Shot of men and women streaming across the bridge, others pouring beneath the arch. All Russia seems to be rising against the Czar.

Cut to a shot of the *Potemkin*. "The enemy has been dealt a decisive blow!" a civilian tells the assembled sailors. "Together with the rising workers of our land we will be victorious!" The sailors fling their white caps in the air, cheering. Cut to a shot of the Odessa Steps, a huge stairway leading down to the harbor, where a crowd has gathered to stare across the water at the *Potemkin*. The sun is shining now, and many women shield themselves with parasols. Cut back to the *Potemkin*, where a forked flag is being raised as a symbol of successful rebellion . . . Fade out.

Part Four: "The Odessa Steps" is probably the most

celebrated sequence ever filmed. The structure of the section clearly exemplifies Eisenstein's theory of dialectical movement. At the start of "The Odessa Steps," the film-maker establishes his "thesis" by cutting back and forth between the happy crowd on shore and the victorious sailors aboard the *Potemkin*. When the foot soldiers and Cossacks appear to put down the demonstration on shore, Eisenstein introduces the "antithesis." In response to the slaughter on the Steps, however, the sailors of the *Potemkin* fire their cannons at the headquarters of the attackers. This represents the "synthesis."

To film the massacre on the Odessa Steps, Eisenstein developed a number of strategies. He built a trolley for his camera on the Steps, so that it could move along with the action. In addition, he wanted to balance the objective presentation of the carnage with subjective shots. To do this, he strapped a camera to the waist of a technician and had him roll down the steps.

One test of a great director is how well he handles crowd scenes. Eisenstein was not only a master of orchestration where large numbers of people were concerned but he also had a genius for isolating individuals in the crowd in order to prevent the audience from merely being overwhelmed by the massive destruction. For example, in "The Odessa Steps" sequence he cuts back and forth between shots showing the soldiers shooting into the crowd and shots depicting the reactions of various persons in the crowd: a mother and her child, a student, a woman wearing pince-nez, a baby in a carriage. By showing us specific human beings up close, by forcing us to identify with them, Eisenstein makes us react emotionally to the sequence. "The Odessa Steps" is no dehumanized newsreel account of an atrocity—it is the high point of Eisenstein's artistry.

From beginning to end, the massacre on the Odessa Steps is masterly in its construction. The transition from the happy scene on the Steps to violence is abrupt and signaled by a title card with one word printed on it: "Suddenly . . ." Shot of a woman's dark hair which fills the screen. The woman pulls back from the camera, still caught in a close-up, her mouth open, screaming. Shot of a legless man hopping in panic down the Steps on blocks of wood held in his hands under his hips. Shots of the crowd fleeing down the Steps. Shot of the cripple gazing for a moment in horror up the Steps. Long shot of the crowd, with the camera positioned at the top of the Steps, the backs of the citizens all that can be seen. There is a bronze statue in the foreground of the shot . . . Then, all at once, we finally see the cause of the panic. Moving underneath the outstretched arms of the statue is a line of soldiers, fixed bayonets on their rifles.

Throughout the massacre on the Steps, Eisenstein uses the various forms of conflict and methods of montage which he discusses in his theoretical writings. There is, for example, graphic conflict (shot of a body intersecting the Steps) and conflict of planes (shot of a line of soldiers shooting down the Steps at a mother holding a child in her arms). Within individual compositions there is conflict between the chaotic rush of the crowd and the mechanical, ordered movement of the soldiers; between light and shadow; between a lone mother moving up the Steps and the crowd fleeing down the Steps past her. As noted earlier, Eisenstein cites the sequence on the Steps as an example of rhythmic montage. The cutting is fast; it is not synchronized with the marching feet of the soldiers. "The final pull of tension," Eisenstein writes, "is supplied by the transfer from the rhythm of the descending feet to another rhythm—a new kind of downward movement—the next intensity level of the same activity—the baby carriage rolling down the Steps. The carriage functions as a directly progressing accelerator of the advancing feet. The stepping descent passes into a rolling descent."[6]

As he did in Part One: "Men and Maggots," in the scene where the sailor breaks the plate on which is inscribed: "Give us this day our daily bread," Eisenstein again expands real time into filmic time in order to emphasize the importance of the slaughter by the Czarist forces. It would take about two minutes for the average person to run down the Odessa Steps. In *Potemkin*, it takes the soldiers almost ten minutes to clear the Steps, because Eisenstein keeps intercutting to show isolated bits of action in conjunction with an overall view of the massacre. Furthermore, time is expanded because Eisenstein presents the same event more than once. At one point, the Steps are swept clean of all the living as the soldiers march relentlessly forward, their rifles smoking. Then a woman carrying her child moves up the Steps to confront the seemingly inhuman soldiers. She is shot down. Once again, the Steps are filled with people and the soldiers are firing at them. We are so involved in the action, however, that during a viewing of *Potemkin* we never ask ourselves where the second wave of people have come from. We simply accept the fact—emotionally—that for the people trapped on the Steps the carnage seems to be going on and on and on. Eisenstein's expansion of time and violation of logic are perfectly justified aesthetically.

The slaughter on the Steps ends with an excellent illustration of what Eisenstein means by montage. Shot of a Cossack swinging his sword, his eyes looking down into the camera. Three more rapid shots—all close-ups—of the Cossack's snarling face. Then a shot of an old woman wearing pince-nez, in close-up, blood spurting from her right eye. We never see the sword as it strikes the eye. Through "shock attraction," Eisenstein takes shots of the Cossack and a shot of the woman—shots which in themselves are "single in meaning"—and combines them to form a new concept: the woman has been slashed by the Cossack.

Immediately, Eisenstein cuts from the woman to the guns of the *Potemkin*. The rebellious sailors fire upon the Odessa Theater, in which the Czar's officers are housed. Once again, Eisenstein provides a memorable example of montage. Three quick shots of marble lions appear on the screen: the first lion is sleeping; the second waking up; the third rising. Individually, the shots are "neutral in content," but the sum of the shots— through the illusion of a single lion jumping to its feet— produces a new idea: the Russian masses are fighting back against the inhumanity of the Czarist government.

"Meeting the Squadron"—the fifth and last part of *Potemkin*—is inevitably a letdown after "The Odessa Steps."

However, Eisenstein does his best to end the film in a dramatic way. Suspense is achieved by establishing the possibility that the bulk of the Russian fleet will sink the *Potemkin*. In order to build up tension, Eisenstein edits dozens of shots of the sailors waiting, water splashing against the ship, the dark sky, dials on pressure gauges, the guns of the *Potemkin*. Sudenly the tension is broken—the squadron is sighted—and activity commences. The sailors of the *Potemkin* prepare themselves for combat, knowing that they are doomed if their fellow seamen on the other ships decide to follow orders. Title: "Will they fire . . ." Eisenstein cuts to the faces of anxious men aboard the *Potemkin*. Title: ". . . or . . ." Cut to shots of more faces, pistons moving furiously below deck. And then, finally, the title: "Brothers!" The sailors aboard the opposing vessels refuse to fire on the *Potemkin*. Overjoyed, the rebellious sailors, cheering, toss their caps in the air. The film ends with a close shot of the *Potemkin's* prow heading straight into the camera, and continuing on to freedom.

One can see that the structure of *Potemkin* also illustrates Eisenstein's concept of progression according to the dialectic. The sailors and the civilian population revolt against authority. This is the "thesis." In response, the government shoots down the civilians on the Odessa Steps. Here we have the "antithesis." Finally, the Russian fleet refuses to fire on the *Potemkin* and allows it to escape unharmed. The massacre has created an even stronger solidarity. This is the "synthesis."

After more than fifty years, *Potemkin* still represents an unforgettable cinematic experience. Vividly photographed by Eduard Tisse (one of the greatest cameramen in the history of cinema), brilliantly conceived and edited by Eisenstein, strong in content, the film has lost none of its power to delight our eyes with its pictorial compositions or hold our attention with its violent actions. The massacre on the Odessa Steps remains an unsurpassable accomplishment.

Eisenstein's conception of himself as both a film artist and a propagandist for the Russian Revolution creates, however, an uneasy tension in *Potemkin*. For example, the characters are over-simplified representations of humanity; they are black (the officers on the ships) and white (the sailors and the workers). At times, *Potemkin* comes perilously close to resembling a cartoon strip, with the "good guys" battling the "bad guys." Joseph Goebbels, propaganda director under Hitler, looked upon Eisenstein's film as a model which Germany would have to surpass . . . a sentiment which prepared the way for Leni Riefenstahl's *Triumph of the Will* (1934), which celebrates the annual Nazi Reich Party Day rally in Nuremberg.

In his essays, Eisenstein often speaks of realism and reality. Unfortunately, he never defines his terms. At the survival level, "reality" seems to be whatever Marx and Engels and Lenin and Stalin say it is. At the artistic level, "reality" is merely something to be put into montage form to fit the revolutionary aims of the film-maker. Truth here is totally dependent on the purposes of the artist, since it is just *as if* things did not exist at all. Now, every artist in cinema transforms reality; he creates, for instance, a new filmic space and time. However, a film like, say, Fellini's *La Strada*, though it reflects the artist's rearrangement of life—that is, his subjectivity (*not* subjectivism)—nonetheless remains a window on the real world. The artist's ideas and attitudes coexist with a reality which—except at the submoral or subethical level—is no mere unspecified stuff.

According to Eisenstein, film can only become art through montage. We know, however, that when a director (for instance, Hitchcock) plans every shot in advance of filming, when, during filming, the shot is lighted this way, composed that way, the actors placed thus and so, artistry is involved in the entire process. Eisenstein tended to place too much stress on the conceptual work of editing, while insufficiently emphasizing *what* the camera sees. "*Primo*: photo-fragments of nature are recorded; *secundo*: these fragments are combined in various ways," he writes. "Thus, the shot (or frame), and thus, montage . . . The minimum 'distortable' fragment of nature is the shot; ingenuity in its combinations is montage.''[7] Because the shot does not distort the real world as much as montage, Eisenstein attaches less significance to it.

We turn now to a film classic which, in its artistry, represents an alternative to Eisenstein's approach in *Potemkin*.

2
Citizen Kane
1941

Like *Potemkin*, Orson Welles's *Citizen Kane* has also often been called "the greatest film ever made." And like *Potemkin*, *Citizen Kane* is certainly *one* of the greatest films ever made. Welles not only directed this masterpiece but also played the leading role—that of Charles Foster Kane. *Citizen Kane*, however, is far from being a one-man show. Herman J. Mankiewicz's contribution to the screenplay was at least as important as Welles's. The cinematographer was Gregg Toland, one of the most highly esteemed technicians who has ever worked in America. Mark Robson and Robert Wise—two men who later became film-makers themselves—were the editors. Bernard Herrmann—whose name appears repeatedly in lists of credits for distinguished films—composed the music. And, finally, the cast includes first-rate stage actors whom Welles brought with him to Hollywood from his Mercury Theater: Joseph Cotten, Everett Sloane, Dorothy Comingore, Agnes Moorehead, George Coulouris, Paul Stewart, and others. But it was Welles who performed the magic which brought all the elements together to create a film classic.

Partly based on the life of publisher William Randolph Hearst—and including his liaison with actress Marion Davies—*Citizen Kane* is a film very much in the modern narrative tradition. The first picture that Welles had intended to make was an adaptation of *Heart of Darkness* by Joseph Conrad, who as a novelist pioneered the technique of telling a story from different points of view. Welles had planned to play Kurtz and have a subjective camera play Marlowe. Although Welles's *Heart of Darkness* never reached the screen, the film-maker adapted Conrad's technique in *Citizen Kane*. Five people tell the audience about Kane. As Welles said once: "They tell five different stories, each biased, so that the truth about Kane, like the truth about any man, can only be calculated, by the sum of everything that has been said about him."[1] This description of point of view in *Citizen Kane* might also be applied to Conrad's *Lord Jim*.

Structure and point of view in *Citizen Kane* are, then, complex. The structure is both horizontal and vertical. Beginning with the death of Kane, at the age of seventy-six, the film goes back in time in an attempt to understand the man's life and actions. What provides the motivation for this flashback technique is the dying word of Kane: "Rosebud!" A reporter named Thompson sets out on a search to unravel the mystery of a word about which the public record of the dead man says nothing. This kind of detective story structure (similar too, in some respects, to Sophocles' *Oedipus*), which moves forward in present time, provides the horizontal dimension of the form. Each of the flashbacks break the forward progression of the story, however, and thus represent the vertical side of the structure.

The form of *Citizen Kane* is also circular. Welles begins the film with shots of Xanadu—a castle-like house which Kane had built in Florida—seen in a long shot from outside. Using dissolves to mark the transitions between shots, the film-maker takes the viewer even closer to the house, until the camera is inside. At the end, Welles moves outside the house again, the shots repeated, with some variation, in reverse order. The camera focuses on a sign which reads: "No Trespassing"—and the film concludes. If we consider point of view in *Citizen Kane* more closely, we will understand the rationale behind Welles's visual and structural approach at the beginning and the end of the film.

During the opening of the picture, we see the bedridden

Kane holding in his hand a glass ball with a snow scene inside. "Rosebud!" murmurs Kane—and dying, he lets the ball roll out of his hand. Although five people tell Kane's story to Thompson, there are actually six flashbacks or six viewpoints on him within the film.* Immediately after the death scene, Welles shows us "News on the March" (a clever parody of "The March of Time"), a newsreel summation of Kane's public life. Here we are given the facts about the central character: how his mother, Mary Kane (Agnes Moorehead), was left a deed to a mine shaft by a defaulting boarder, and how she became rich as a result; how Walter P. Thatcher (George Coulouris), a banker, became the guardian of young Kane; how Kane went on to become an influencial publisher and a powerful man; how Thatcher condemned the adult Kane as a Fascist; how Kane married a president's niece, Emily Norton (Ruth Warrick), who left him in 1916, and who two years later was killed in an automobile accident with their son; how, two weeks after his divorce, Kane married a "singer" named Susan Alexander (Dorothy Comingore); how Kane's first marriage and political career had been smashed when his liaison with Susan had first been disclosed; how Kane built an opera house for his second wife, and also Xanadu; how Kane lost control of his newspapers in 1929; and how, finally, he had died, alone in Xanadu.

During the newsreel, we glimpse all the witness-as-narrator characters, with the exception of Raymond (Paul Stewart), who was Kane's butler in his last years. In addition to Thatcher (the first narrator after the newsreel), Susan (the fourth), and Raymond (the last), there is Bernstein (Everett Sloan) and Jedediah Leland (Joseph Cotten), the second and third narrators respectively.

"All we saw on that screen," says Rawlston, the publisher of a news magazine and producer of the newsreel, "was a big American." Thompson then goes on his search for the meaning

---

* There is, of course, a seventh viewpoint on Kane—the viewer's—but it is not within the film.

of "Rosebud"—hoping to find the truth about the private man behind the public image.

Thompson visits an Atlantic City nightclub owned by Susan Alexander, and after finding her unwilling to talk about her relationship with Kane, he next goes to the Thatcher Memorial Library. There the reporter reads the late Thatcher's unpublished memoirs in an attempt to get his point of view on Kane. As Thompson reads, Welles dissolves into a shot of young Kane, aged five, playing in the snow outside his mother's boardinghouse. In this scene, we see how reluctant the boy is to leave his childhood home, and the love and warmth of his mother's presence. But his mother believes that what she is doing will benefit her son. Before departing, young Kane strikes Thatcher in the stomach with his sled. The scene ends with a medium shot of the house, the snow falling, the sled covered with snow . . . Dissolve to a shot of Thatcher wishing young Kane a Merry Christmas and giving him a new sled—which the boy rejects, because it is not the one he left behind.

In the remainder of the Thatcher flashback, we see the adult Kane in opposition to the interests of Thatcher and his plutocratic-minded friends. Young Kane, who owns a newspaper called the *Inquirer*, acknowledges to Thatcher a split in his feelings about businessmen. As a businessman himself, he considers the owner of the *Inquirer* an enemy of his class; but as the owner of the *Inquirer*, he feels it is his job to protect the poor from the exploitation of the rich. Before the flashback ends, we view an older Kane losing his newspapers in 1929, although not his great wealth. Instead of investing his money, Kane had always used it "to buy things." "You know," says Kane, "if I hadn't been very rich, I might have been a really great man." When Thatcher asks Kane what he would like to have been, Kane replies: "Everything you hate." At this point, Thompson closes the manuscript.

Next Thompson visits Bernstein—Kane's former general manager—who tells the reporter that the word "Rosebud" means nothing to him. But he does suggest that "Rosebud" might be associated with something far back in time, something which other people might consider trivial. Kane was hard to understand, Bernstein admits. "It wasn't money he wanted," he says. During the Bernstein flashback, the viewer sees young Kane taking over the *Inquirer* with great enthusiasm. Leland is impressed with Kane's Declaration of Principles: "I will provide the people of this city with a daily newspaper that will tell all the news honestly; I will also provide them with a fighting and tireless champion of their rights as citizens and as human beings." In order to sell papers, however, Kane adopts the tactics of a scandal sheet. He also woos over to his paper the entire staff of the *Chronicle*, a rival daily. Leland begins to become disenchanted with Kane when he realizes that the *Chronicle* staff was formerly as devoted to that paper's policies as they now profess to be to the *Inquirer's*. He is afraid that the new men might change Kane's way of thinking. What Leland cannot yet admit, even to himself, is his fear that Kane might not have any real abiding principles—only a vast egotism. Bernstein, however, sees Kane as both a shrewd businessman and an idealist.

Thompson's visit to Leland—Kane's former friend and a former critic on the *Inquirer*—who is in a hospital, carries the Kane story farther along, but brings it no closer to a solution of the "Rosebud" mystery. In this section, we witness the deterioration of Kane's first marriage and his meeting with Susan. According to Leland, what motivated Kane throughout his life was a search for love. He had none to give, however, except to himself and probably to his mother. As Leland sees it, Kane went into politics because he wanted the voters to love him; but the scandal involving Susan turned the public against him. Bitter over Kane's loss of virtue, Leland asks Kane to transfer him to a Chicago paper. In his own bitterness, Kane turns away from politics and attempts to make the public accept Susan as an opera star. He fails again. And when Susan sings in Chicago, Leland pans her in his review—a review which he is too drunk to finish, but which Kane finishes for him. Kane then fires Leland, and that ends their friendship. Leland tells Thompson that Kane was just trying to prove he was an honest man in finishing the review. "He was always trying to prove something," he says. Kane built Xanadu—a world within a world—because he was disappointed with reality.

When Thompson revisits Susan, she is willing to talk to him—but not about "Rosebud." Her view of Kane is similar to Leland's. Kane drove her to be a singer against her will. It was only when she had attempted suicide that he allowed her to quit her opera career. In a flashback, we see Kane telling Susan: "Whatever I do, I do because I love you;" to which she replies: "You don't love me. You want me to love you." Bored and restless in Xanadu, Susan finally leaves Kane. Looking back on the dead man, now, she feels sorry for him.

The viewpoint on Kane given by Raymond, his former butler, takes up where Susan's ends. We again see the parting between Kane and Susan, but this time we also see Kane smashing everything in his wife's room. Finally, Kane picks up a glass ball with snow inside of it, and whispers: "Rosebud." Thompson is not satisfied that Raymond has told him very much. As the butler sees Kane, the dead man was simply a queer old man whose mutterings did not mean anything.

At the end of the film, Thompson has still not solved the mystery of "Rosebud." The scene is the basement of Xanadu, where all of Kane's vast possessions are stored. Some "junk" is being burned in a furnace. Thompson tells an associate: "Mr. Kane was a man who got everything he wanted, and then lost it. Maybe 'Rosebud' was something he couldn't get or something he lost. Anyway, it wouldn't have explained anything. I don't think any word can explain a man's life."

Shot of a sled burning in the furnace. On the sled we can read the word: "Rosebud."

The ending of *Citizen Kane*, like the film itself, is complex. We must balance what Thompson says—"I don't think any word can explain a man's life"—against the word: "Rosebud"—which suggests that all his life Kane suffered from the traumatic experience of being separated from his mother and his childhood home. (The glass ball with snow inside of it, of course, reinforces this symbolism.) Point of view, structure, and the visual approach in *Citizen Kane* also emphasize complexity, whereas an anecdote Bernstein tells Thompson again suggests simplicity: "One day, back in 1896, I was crossing over to Jersey on the ferry, and as we pulled out, there was another ferry pulling in, and on it there was a girl waiting to get off. A white dress she had on. She was carrying a white parasol. I only saw her for one second. She didn't see me at all, but I'll bet a month hasn't gone by since that I haven't thought of that girl."

At the end, we are still left with a sense of mystery. The opening shots move into Xanadu in an attempt to bring us to an understanding of a man's life. But just as we seem to have found the clue which had escaped Thompson, Welles shows us smoke curling from the chimney of Xanadu, and the camera moves outside again, closing with a shot on the "No Trespassing" sign. The clue—or clues—to Kane's life have gone up in smoke. We seem to be left with the thought: One should not try to fully comprehend the mystery of any man's existence.

In its use of visual techniques, *Citizen Kane* is brilliant. The newsreel sequence, for example, has the look of old prints. The earliest shots are jerky in rhythm, the film scratched and grainy. Later in the flashback sequences, however, we see some of the same shots in a non-jerky rhythm, unscratched and clear. When Welles shifts to the projection room after the newsreel, he keeps the men's faces, for the most part, in darkness, with light glowing in windows around them. In this way, the film-maker forces us to listen to what the men have to say—here the words are more important than the faces—but we listen while looking at a visually interesting screen.

When Thompson goes to visit Susan at her nightclub for the first time, Welles opens on a shot of a billboard picture of the woman illuminated by lightning; then the camera travels up, through the rain, to the roof of the building; then, on another flash of lightning, there is a cut and the camera is past the glass skylight and inside the club, looking down on Susan, who is drunkenly sobbing, alone. Aside from the exciting way in

Charles Foster Kane (Orson Welles) making a speech at a political rally, from *Citizen Kane*. Note the juxtaposition of Kane's face at left in close-up with the medium shot of Kane at center in the foreground.

25

which Welles's camera slowly approaches Susan, the final high-angle shot characterizes her fallen state. Once the wife of a rich and famous man, she is now reduced to singing in a cheap nightclub she has established.

Inside the Thatcher Memorial Library, an immense beam of light falls across the table at which Thompson is seated, transforming the room into a parody of a church. As the reporter reads Thatcher's memoirs concerning his first meeting with the boy Kane, Welles uses a dissolve from the white page of the manuscript to the white snow of the yard in front of the boardinghouse.

When Kane buys the writers from the *Chronicle*, Welles shows us a picture of the *Chronicle* staff in the window of that newspaper's office; then his camera tracks in closer to the picture; there is a dissolve to the interior of the *Inquirer*'s office—and now we see the same men, in the same shot as in the previous still, suddenly animated, six years later.

Leland's flashback is introduced in a striking manner. Shot of Leland, telling Thompson about Emily, Kane's first wife. Slowly, Welles superimposes over Leland a shot of the Kane's breakfast table. He holds the superimposition for a moment—then fades out the image of Leland. What follows is one of the most remarked upon scenes in the entire film. The collapse of Kane's first marriage is shown in a time-span covering years but shot and recorded as though in a single conversation—moving from loving words through heated arguments to bitter silence (Kane reading the *Inquirer*, Emily the *Chronicle*!). Welles alternates close shots of Kane with close shots of Emily, employing swing dissolves for the transitions. The movement back to present time with Leland in the hospital balances the opening. Over the shot of the silent breakfast table scene, Welles fades in a picture of old Leland again. Finally, he fades out the shot of the Kanes, thus ending the superimposition, and focuses entirely on Leland.

One of the most famous traveling shots in the film occurs while Susan is singing on the stage. As the poor woman struggles through her number—*"Tu m'as trop entendu"*—Welles's camera begins moving up to the top of the set. Finally it stops and focuses on two stagehands sitting on a catwalk, gazing down. One man turns, looks at the other, and silently holds his nose.

But surely, the most thrilling moving camera shots in *Citizen Kane* occur at the end. After Thompson's speech about "Rosebud," Welles's camera tracks over the enormous pile of crated "things" Kane had bought over the years—bought to fill the void created by his inability to love and by whatever else eluded him in life. Through a series of dissolves, the moving camera draws ever closer to the belongings of Kane's mother . . . until it reaches the sled.

Welles's use of sound is similarly outstanding. Thatcher remarks to the boy Kane, "Well, Charles, Merry Christmas;" to which the lad replies, "Merry Christmas." Then, as Thatcher's voice continues with, "And a Happy New Year," we have jumped ahead to Kane's twenty-first birthday. Throughout the picture, Welles uses this kind of overlapping sound for bridging transitions between scenes set in the present and for jumping ahead in time during the flashback sections. Welles called this technique "lightning mixes." Shot of Susan playing the piano for Kane in her run-down flat; dissolve to a shot of her, still playing the same piece, but at another piano, and in a more fashionable apartment. Kane applauds . . . dissolve again to a crowd applauding as Leland addresses them on Kane's behalf. Leland says: "There is only one man who can rid the politics of this state of evil domination of Boss Jim Gettys . . . I am speaking of Charles Foster Kane, the fighting liberal, the friend of the workingman, the next governor of this state, who entered upon this campaign . . ." Cut to a close-up of a rally poster with Kane's picture on it; camera pans down to Kane, who, speaking to a different crowd, finishes Leland's speech: ". . . with one purpose only . . . to point out and make public the dishonesty, the downright villainy of Boss Jim Gettys's political machine."

Citizen Kane is filled with ironic juxtapositions of sound and image. When Kane has a party in which he celebrates hiring the *Chronicle* staff for his own paper, we see girls dancing with fake guns, everyone laughing, and Kane saying: "Well, gentlemen, are we going to declare war on Spain, or are we not?" Later in the film, Susan criticizes Kane for firing Leland after the latter wrote a bad review of her singing, and at the same time giving his old friend a parting gift of a $25,000 check. As Susan berates Kane, we see him examine the check which Leland has returned, torn in pieces. Near the end of the film, Kane and Susan quarrel in a tent; outside the tent, a black entertainer sings: "It can't be love . . . For there is no true love." When Susan leaves Kane, Raymond's flashback begins with a shot of a cockatoo shrieking—the sound echoing the shrill voice of the departing wife.

Welles's background in radio enabled him to bring a distinct sensitivity to sound effects. In order to emphasize the spaciousness of Xanadu, and at the same time to underline the emptiness of Kane's life there with Susan, he used an echo box or chamber. The voice of the narrator of the newsreel remains strident, whereas the voices in the Thatcher Memorial Library sound hollow, in a way reminiscent of Xanadu.

The aspect of *Citizen Kane* which has probably occasioned the most discussion is Welles's use of deep-focus photography; that is, a focus in which all objects from close foreground to distant background are seen in sharp definition. Although deep-focus had been used sporadically in earlier films by other directors—most notably by Jean Renoir in *Boudu Saved from Drowning* (1932), *Toni* (1934), and *The Rules of the Game* (1939)—Welles seems to have been the first film-maker to employ the technique consistently in a single film. When Peter Bogdanovich asked Welles why he used so much deep-focus shooting in *Citizen Kane*, the director replied: "Well, in life you see everything in focus at the same time, so why not in the movies?" ("The Kane Mutiny," *Esquire*, October 1972, p. 184).

When, during the Thatcher flashback, young Kane's fate is decided, Welles uses deep-focus. In the foreground, we see the

Kane and Susan (Dorothy Comingore) at Xanadu. Susan, in order to over-come her boredom, works on a jigsaw puzzle, a diversion that mirrors the structure of *Citizen Kane*. Each narrator provides a piece of the puzzle that makes up Kane's life.

mother, father, and Thatcher—and in the background, through the window, we see the boy enjoying himself for the last time in the snow. Whereas Eisenstein would have cut back and forth between the adults inside the house and the boy outside in order to make the relationship clear, Welles gives us simultaneity in one shot.

During the scene in which Kane finishes the bad review of Susan's singing begun by the drunken Leland, Welles again uses deep-focus imaginatively. Shot of Kane in the foreground, seated at a typewriter, with Leland in the background, walking shakily towards the camera. Similarly, when Susan's voice teacher is exasperatedly attempting to instruct her in one scene, Welles also employs deep-focus. In the foreground, we see Susan and the maestro at the piano; in the background, unseen by both, we see Kane enter the room. Slowly—like Leland in the scene previously described—Kane makes his way forward, toward Susan and her teacher, toward the camera, toward the viewer. In both scenes, the gradual approach of the character, steadily kept in clear focus, dramatically prepares the viewer for a confrontation.

When Susan tries to kill herself after still another bad performance, Welles presents a three-level deep-focus shot: close up we see a glass and a bottle of poison; at midpoint we see Susan's face against a bed pillow; and in the background we see a crack of light underneath the door. We hear Susan wheezing, and Kane outside knocking hard. André Bazin has written: "The dramatic structure of the scene is essentially based on the distinction between the two sounds: the gasps, nearby, of Susan and the bangings of her husband behind the door. A tension is established between these two poles, held at a distance by the depth of focus."[2] Finally, Welles also uses deep-focus in a shot depicting the relationship of Kane and Susan at Xanadu. With the camera placed just behind Kane's head (subjective angle), we see across the immensity of the room Susan, working a jigsaw puzzle, seated near the hearth. The shot not only emphasizes the vastness of the room, but—what is more important—suggests the emotional distance separating husband and wife.

30

In several books, Bazin has argued that deep-focus photography is superior to montage. He divides film-makers into two groups: those who opt for the image and those who prefer the object or reality. A director (like Eisenstein) who puts his faith in the image adds something to reality; the director (like Welles) who chooses the second course allows reality to "speak" for itself. Montage fragments the world; deep-focus preserves the unity of the world. Whereas Eisenstein emphasizes the juxtaposition of frames, Welles stresses the content of a frame. Montage oversimplifies experience by imposing a single, preconceived, arbitrary meaning on events; deep-focus not only provides the viewer with options as to what he will look at in a shot (there are no options in montage), but it also respects the ambiguous nature of reality (there is no room for ambiguity in montage). True, *Citizen Kane* has its artificial or expressionistic side, Bazin admits, but Toland's in-depth photography permits entire scenes to be covered in a single take, the camera remaining still, the actors moving within the frame. Welles's method is based on a concern for the continuity of dramatic space and its duration.

Bazin overstates the case against Eisenstein and montage in favor of Welles and deep-focus. There is room in film for both approaches. If a director wants to make his theme clear, he can guide the viewer's perceptions through the careful use of montage; he can focus attention on essential objects through close-ups, or he can cut to relevant details, thus forcing the viewer to see what he wants him to see. Such an approach should require no apology. Art involves selection; art is reality filtered through, and arranged by, an individual consciousness. Not all film-makers look at either art or reality, however, in the same way. Some artists wish to allow the viewer a greater latitude in interpretation, and hence a higher level of involvement, during the film experience. Deep-focus shooting provides the means for this presentation of screen action.

Montage, if carried to an extreme, is too literary or rhetorical; deep-focus, if overused, is too stagy or theatrical. Neither method, at its best, can lay claim to any necessary or inherent superiority to the other. The argument that deep-focus is more like life remains unconvincing, inasmuch as art is not life. Deep-focus allows background and foreground to interact; in addition, it also permits the viewer to relate the actions. However, the film-maker has arranged such shots so that the viewer *does* make the connections. The action isn't spontaneous. It is the artist who creates the illusion of improvisation, of unrehearsed lifelikeness.

Technique depends on the specific demands of story, character, and theme. Suppose a director wants to show that his hero feels lonely even in a crowd. The scene is a party. Should the director cut back and forth between the various members of the gathering, all of whom are talking and laughing, to the hero, who is seated by himself in a corner? Or should the director choose deep-focus by simply revealing the crowd in the background of the room and the isolated hero in the foreground? Which approach would be better?

No categorical answer is possible. The pace of a particular story may well demand a cutting rhythm. Or a previous pattern of symbolic imagery may require that deep-focus be used. A close inspection of most films today will reveal that a combination of montage and deep-focus has been employed.

Eisenstein in *Potemkin* and Welles in *Citizen Kane* both showed that great films can be made using either approach.

3
The Bicycle Thief
1949

In 1943, the influential Italian film theorist and teacher Umberto Barbaro urged that it was incumbent upon the cinema in his country to show society as it really was, and to be done with musicals and light comedies and similar confections. Barbaro's ideas were at the basis of neo-realism, a major movement in Italian film, which thrived from 1944 to 1952. With Mussolini and Fascism gone, and Italy battered by poverty and disillusionment, the neo-realists proposed that the cinema present an authentic view of the times—and that it cope with social problems.

Ironically enough, neo-realism owes much to the Fascists. In 1935, Mussolini's government founded the Centro Sperimentale, the official film school in Rome, headed by Luigi Chiarini, who also published a journal called *Bianco e Nero*, which later helped spread the neo-realist message. Many technicians, cameramen, and editors were trained at the Centro Sperimentale. In addition, later neo-realist directors like Luigi Zampa, Pietro Germi, Giuseppe De Santis, Roberto Rossellini, and Michelangelo Antonioni attended the school. Then, in 1937, Mussolini built Cinecitta, the biggest film studio in Europe. When Fascism became history, it left behind in Italy a well-trained number of film-makers and production crews, even though during the years it had held power creativity had been smothered. It was time for another Italian Renaissance.

In background, the neo-realist directors were mainly writers or newspapermen. As a group, they were university graduates and middle-class. Ideologically, they were Marxists and left-wing Catholics. From the beginning, the determination of the neo-realists to show conditions in Italy as they really were prompted the government and the Church to react against them. As George Huaco has pointed out, for the neo-realist film-makers "reality" equalled "poverty, unemployment, hunger." Similarly, "people" were the "unemployed, industrial workers, hungry farmers and fishermen, the poverty-stricken and abandoned very young and very old, migrant workers . . . The non-human environment [was] static, deprivational, cruel; its emotional tone [was] a mixture of boredom and hopelessness."[1] Like the Soviet directors of the silent age, the neo-realists used nonprofessional actors. Whether they were filming during the day or night, they favored location shooting and natural lighting. A uniform grayness, appropriate to the subject matter, defines the tone of the neo-realist film.

Of the masterpieces of Italian neo-realism—including Luchino Visconti's *Ossessione* (1943) and *La Terra Trema* (1948), Rossellini's *Open City* (1945) and *Paisan* (1946), Vittorio De Sica's *Shoeshine* (1946) and *Umberto D.* (1951)—perhaps the best-known example remains De Sica's *The Bicycle Thief*.

The Bicycle Thief was written for the screen by Cesare Zavattini, who based his treatment on a novel by Luigi Bartolini. De Sica and Zavattini worked together on many films. "I have the sentiment, the emotion," De Sica told Guy Flatley once. "Zavattini is the cerebral one" (*New York Times*, January 16, 1972). In a 1952 essay entitled "Some Ideas on the Cinema," Zavattini discusses his aesthetic, which is relevant to an understanding of *The Bicycle Thief*.

Most people, Zavattini contends, look upon daily life as a tiresome business. It is boring and uninteresting. As a result, film-makers have always felt the need to invent stories, fables, as substitutes for everyday reality. Neo-realists deny the necessity for such falsification of life. Reality, they argue, is far from dull, and the artist's job consists in making the audience think and feel about what actually exists.

The neo-realist film is the exact opposite of the plotted film—that is, the film in which one event produces another, and so on, in a causal chain, until the happy ending is reached. This approach, according to Zavattini, betrays a suspicion of reality. The neo-realists prefer to create a scene, and then dilate it, in terms of character and theme. Film-makers should not attempt to make audiences believe in the reality of imaginary stories; instead, they should probe reality until the audience sees the meaning of their daily lives. The camera has a "hunger for reality"—no other medium has its ability to show things. But by showing things, Zavattini does not intend that the camera must remain limited to the surfaces of reality. On the contrary, the camera, by lingering upon a scene, has the power of penetrating to life's quiddity. Neo-realism is both a moral and an artistic philosophy.

Neo-realism, Zavattini argues, deals with poverty because poverty remains one of the most important social problems. Neo-realism does not offer solutions because problems remain unresolved in life. Why should the film-maker be obliged to solve all the difficulties of society? Zavattini argues that a film should present life as it is, and make the viewer feel the need for working at solutions. Neo-realism concerns itself with what is normal in life rather than what is exceptional. The moviegoer is the real hero of life, the true protagonist of reality, not some imaginary character in a fabricated story. Neo-realism appeals to what is responsible and dignified in every human being. When we go to the movies, we must identify ourselves with what we are, otherwise we will become alienated from our true selves.[2]

An actor for many years, De Sica directed his first film (*Twenty-Four Roses*) in 1940. He made three more lightweight films before he met Zavattini, who turned him in the direction of neo-realism. Although *Shoeshine* received good reviews, De Sica had trouble obtaining backing for *The Bicycle Thief.* David O. Selznick was interested in the project, but he wanted to cast Cary Grant in the part of Antonio Ricci, the protagonist, who is an Italian laborer. De Sica rejected the offer. Finally, after two years, the film-maker had the necessary capital. He cast a real workingman—Lamberto Maggiorani—as Ricci. After *The Bicycle Thief* appeared, everyone praised Maggiorani's performance. Billy Wilder interviewed him for a picture, but quickly realized that the hero of *The Bicycle Thief* was not really an actor. De Sica had made Maggiorani *seem* to be an actor—thanks to the director's own acting talent. A Roman newsboy—Enzo Staiola—was cast in the role of Ricci's son, Bruno. Staiola never became an actor, either.

De Sica once described his success with nonprofessionals by saying: "I explain and explain, and I am very convincing. I seem to have a special gift for making myself understood by actors. Either I play the part or I explain it, slowly, patiently, with a smile on my face and never any anger."[3]

Although Zavattini's contribution to *The Bicycle Thief* remains important, the film is De Sica's because, as the late film-maker himself also once pointed out, images are more significant than dialogue. If someone else had directed *The Bicycle Thief*, it probably would have had merit—but it would have been different from De Sica's version.[4] The "sentiment" and "emotion" which the warm-hearted De Sica put into *The Bicycle Thief* goes a long way towards explaining its greatness.

Stylistically, *The Bicycle Thief* remains typical of De Sica's work as a director. There is no conspicuous editing technique, such as that which distinguishes Eisenstein's "shock cutting" or montage construction. Nor do we find De Sica using the camera or sound in the manner of Welles. There are no striking camera angles; no swish pans; no wipes; no "lightning mixes." However, like Welles, De Sica tends to present his action in long takes—the camera patiently recording what *seems* like life itself unfolding—but, unlike Welles, the Italian does not use dramatic compositions involving extreme deep-focus. De Sica's is the art which conceals art. His style calls attention, not to itself, but to the subject. Throughout *The Bicycle Thief*, De Sica mixes stationary camera shots with slow tracking shots and

Bruno (Enzo Staiola) looks up admiringly at his father, Antonio Ricci (Lamberto Maggiorani), who has a new job as a bill poster. The bicycle is vital to his job.

slow pans. The effect of this technique is to make the viewer all but unconscious of the mechanics of film-making.

But *The Bicycle Thief* is no mere "slice of life." In spite of what Zavattini has to say about the camera's "hunger for reality," De Sica never believed that film equals reality. It was his conviction that neo-realism means reality transformed into poetry.[5] Precisely how this cinematic magic is accomplished, though, remains the artist's secret.

The Bicycle Thief opens on a Friday. It is sunny and warm. The scene is a government housing project for workers, just outside of Rome. On a staircase, a government official calls out the name: "Ricci . . . Where's Ricci." When Ricci appears, the official tells him that there is a job for him as a bill poster. The unemployed men around Ricci protest to the official that they need work too. De Sica's theme—man's need for human solidarity—is opposed by a social system in which poverty forces men into competition with each other for jobs. In this opening scene, the drab buildings, the crowds of shabbily dressed men, the dry dusty milieu all contribute to the sense of an existence unfit for men, of a system which robs men of their dignity and encourages selfishness. The government official takes refuge behind the usual excuse: "What can I do? Can I help it if there isn't enough work?"

Ricci's problem is that he needs a bicycle for his job as a bill poster, but his bicycle is in a pawnshop. At home, his wife Maria (Lianella Carell) pulls the sheets off their bed and takes new sheets from their dresser, announcing: "We'll sleep without sheets." They go to the pawnshop with the sheets so that they can buy back the bicycle. An employee takes the bundle of linen, walks down an aisle, and climbs up shelf after shelf of pawned sheets, the camera tilting up to follow his progress. It is a memorable shot—driving home the point that the Ricci family are not exceptional in their poverty and desperation.

On the way home, over the protests of her husband, Maria stops at the apartment of a woman fortune teller. To Ricci, the woman is a charlatan. But Maria, who believes in her, makes a donation of fifty lire. "Listen," says Maria, "she said you'd find a job, and you found one." Ricci remains skeptical.

The first time we see Bruno—Ricci's young son—is the following morning. There is a close-up of a bicycle wheel and through the spokes we can see the boy, polishing the vehicle with serious attention. Bruno finds a dent in the bicycle. Although Ricci views it as inconsequential, his son remains angry—not only at those who damaged the vehicle at the pawnshop but also at his father, who did not see it or find fault with the pawnbroker because of it. Throughout *The Bicycle Thief*, Bruno is depicted as a boy-man, and the relationship which develops between father and son is central to the structure and theme of the film.

That morning Ricci and Maria are in a cheerful mood. Maria tells her husband that he looks handsome in his bill poster's uniform. They embrace. But Maria pretends that she does not like Ricci's rough lovemaking. "Go away with you," she says. "You hurt me—and you'll wake the baby." Clearly, a good marriage needs more than love. Without economic security, a couple—no matter how much they care for each other—cannot be happy. The bicycle is vital to Ricci's marriage.

When it is time for Ricci and Bruno to leave for work, De Sica shows us how the boy identifies with his father and, once more, underscores Bruno's incipient maturity. When Ricci takes his package of lunch, he places it in the front pocket of his overalls; Bruno imitates his father by doing the same with his lunch. Then, before leaving the room, Bruno gazes at the baby lying on the bed. He notices that the shutters are open, and he proceeds to close them, in order to keep the sun out of the baby's eyes. Now that Ricci has a job, Bruno—like his mother—loves and respects his father more than ever. He demonstrates this not only through imitation but also through his sense of responsibility.

Outside De Sica's camera shows us Ricci riding with Bruno sitting on the handlebars of the bicycle. The street is filled with other cyclists. At the spot where Ricci leaves Bruno a bus stops and a large number of persons exit. Throughout *The Bicycle Thief*, De Sica fills the screen with masses of people. Everywhere there is overcrowding, vast poverty, a struggle for existence, indifference. Against this dreary backdrop the love between father and son, and between husband and wife, shines brightly.

Shot of Ricci attempting to put up a poster of Rita Hayworth as Gilda,* but not succeeding very well. Air bubbles appear all over the poster. When Charles Thomas Samuels asked De Sica why he used this particular poster, the filmmaker replied: "Because [Gilda] is so far away from [Ricci's] world, and he clumsily ruins this image of that woman."[6] While Ricci is struggling with a romanticized likeness of a famous movie star, real thieves are proceeding to steal his bicycle. As one thief rides off on the bike, a second pretends to inadvertently get in Ricci's way, thus temporarily blocking his pursuit. The camera pans with Ricci as he chases the thief riding the bicycle into a piazza. "Thief! Thief!" shouts Ricci—but no one in the crowded square tries to help him apprehend the culprit. Ricci jumps on the running board of a passing car and instructs the driver to give chase. But the second thief jumps on the opposite running board, deliberately giving the driver wrong directions. The bicycle thief escapes.

At the police station, Ricci's misfortune is treated routinely. There remains the same bureaucratic inefficiency and indifference that prevailed earlier in the opening of the film, at the government housing project, when the official was unable to provide jobs for most of the unemployed men. "People saw what happened to my bike," Ricci tells the police officer, "but nobody cared." Neither does Failoni, the policemen, who tells Ricci to look for the stolen vehicle himself: "We'd need an entire mobile brigade to find your bicycle." When a newspaper reporter passes Failoni, he asks: "Anything new, officer?"; to which the officer replies: "No, nothing . . . just a bicycle." Ricci is crushed.

---

* *Gilda* (1946), directed by Charles Vidor.

The Bicycle Thief 1949

That night Ricci, who had been ashamed to tell Bruno that the bicycle was stolen—"It's broken," he had said—goes to the housing project for help. A communist agitator is speaking in one area: "It's impossible to find jobs for people, since there's no work. We, as a cell, have pointed this out to the Labor Office. The dole isn't the answer . . . "* Ricci is looking for a man named Biaocco. "We are constantly trying to integrate you into the system," the communist continues, "but you can't expect miracles." In another area of the project, the workers are rehearsing a silly play in an amateurish fashion. The foolish spectacle contrasts with the sadness of Ricci in search of his stolen bike. He asks Biaocco for help, and the latter suggests that their only chance is to go to the Piazza Vittorio early in the morning, because thieves sell stolen vehicles right away. Just then, Maria enters. Ricci had been afraid to go home that evening because he did not want to hear her comments about the stolen bicycle. He feels that he has lost the respect of his wife and son.

Sunday morning. In a long shot we see the Piazza Vittorio, dimly in the morning light. Ricci and Bruno, who has by this time been told about the theft, emerge from a bus, locate Biaocco and two other men, and the search for the bicycle commences. About twenty minutes into this film which runs for eighty-seven minutes, then, a variation of that staple of movie construction—the chase—helps determine its form. Biaocco assumes that the bike has already been broken down; they will have to look for the parts. When Bruno remembers that the bicycle had a Fides frame, he wins the admiration of his father and the other men. The group separate so that each of them can search for a different part. Unhappily, they are unable to find the stolen bicycle.

"Why not try Porta Portes?" Biaocco suggest to Ricci. "Maniconi can drive you there. We'll stay here . . . "

* "There is a misunderstanding about my politics," De Sica told Guy Flatley. "The theme of my serious work is the Christian theme of human solidarity. I am very concerned with poverty, and my movies deal with poor, oppressed people. I *defend* them, but that does not make me a communist. I have never been a communist. I am not a member of any political party."

41

Suddenly the sky grows dark. Shot of a truck, moving down an empty road. Maniconi, Ricci, and Bruno are seated in the front seat. It begins to rain. De Sica places his camera behind the men, so that we gaze out through the windshield as they do, thus identifying with them. The rain turns into a deluge. Nevertheless, Ricci and Bruno get out of the truck and run towards the stalls of the market. Maniconi drives off. Visually, this is one of the most powerful moments in the film. The rain creates a scene of total disorder: there are shots of vendors covering up their merchandise; people running for cover in all directions; cyclists riding by, some of them—ironically— carting an extra bike. Ricci and Bruno walk dazedly in the rain. Thoughout *The Bicycle Thief*, Alessandro Cicognini's music is often obtrusive, overly insistent, calling attention to itself, and thus working at odds with the realism of the film.* In this scene, however, the swelling music blends effectively with the rain and the chaos and the growing sense of helplessness Ricci and Bruno feel.

Finally the rain stops. And as it does, Ricci sees a young man who resembles the thief talking to an old man, and then passing some money to him. The thief rides off on his bicycle. As he had done the day before, Ricci shouts: "Thief! Thief!" Again, however, no one seems to care. Ricci chases the thief, but he soon gives up. Instead, he turns back to the old man. "I don't know anything," the old man insists. All the same, Ricci and Bruno follow him into a church.

In the scene which follows, Di Sica incurred the anger of the Roman Catholic Church by showing, in a serio-comic fashion, the inept manner in which social problems can be treated in the name of Christ. Inside the vestibule of the church, a well-dressed man is giving a poor wretch a shave, while an arrogant society woman acts patronizingly toward those who need help. The old man whom Ricci and Bruno have pursued into the church has come for a meal, but the lady informs him that before eating he must sit through a mass.

---

* "I am against music," De Sica remarked once, ". . . but the producers always insist on it."[7]

Ricci has found the person who stole his bicycle. The thief's friends, however, protect him and threaten Ricci.

As Ricci and Bruno enter the interior of the church, we hear the "Ave Maria" played on an organ. Contrast is one of the most powerful techniques De Sica uses in *The Bicycle Thief*. The inefficiency of the bureaucracy is contrasted with the desperation of unemployed workers; the abstract rhetoric of the communists is contrasted with the concrete tragedy of individual lives; the condescending, heartless charity of those who represent the Church is contrasted with the resentment and indifference of the poor who want not "pie in the sky" but food in their bellies and a sense of self-respect.

Contrast is also an important element in the mass scene. Ricci sits next to the old man and tries to get him to inform on the thief. As De Sica cuts back and forth between the two men—Ricci struggling for his right to earn his daily bread—a prosperous layman is leading the congregation in a beautiful but irrelevant prayer "I want to leave this holy place with a pure soul and a peace of mind. I try again to overcome the weakness of my flesh . . . " Finally, the old man slips away from Ricci and Bruno, and disappears from the church.

Outside Bruno criticizes his father for allowing the old man to escape. Weary and frustrated, Ricci slaps his son in the face. He is immediately sorry but does not know how to repair the injury. Bruno, who is also tired and unhappy, reacts to the blow by dropping his adult pose and becoming the child he is: "You're horrible . . . I'm going to tell Mama!" Ricci and Bruno have been close throughout the film; now their plight has driven them apart. De Sica visually emphasizes their alienation from each other by having Ricci walk along in the foreground of the shot, with Bruno sulkily keeping up with him—parallel to him—in the background.

Ricci instructs Bruno to wait for him on a bridge while he searches for the old man. Presently Ricci hears voices off camera: "Over there—someone's drowning . . . He's fallen in." Fearful that it is Bruno the voices refer to, Ricci rushes toward the water, calling his son's name, his own voice echoing under the arch of the bridge. Relieved to discover the body now on shore is not that of his son, Ricci gazes up to the top of the bridge, where Bruno remains obediently waiting, oblivious to his father's concern.

In order to regain his son's affection, Ricci takes Bruno to an expensive cafe. When Ricci—who had to count his money before entering—asks for a pizza, the snobbish waiter replies: "This is a restaurant, not a pizzeria." Ricci orders a meal. Although Ricci seems out of place here, Bruno's face registers admiration and love for his father again. The boy's happiness increases when Ricci pours him a glass of wine. "If your mother only knew I was allowing you to drink!" says Ricci. Once more, little Bruno feels like a man. And Ricci—though concerned about the cost of the meal, as well as his bleak future if he does not retrieve the bicycle—consoles himself with the thought: "Everything sorts itself out, except death."

Afterward, however, Ricci's desperation prompts him to visit the same fortune teller Maria had gone to see—the one whom Ricci, when he had a job, had called a fake. The woman profoundly observes: "Either you will find your bicycle immediately or you will never find it." Showing his displeasure, Ricci pays the fortune teller's assistant, and exits.

Outside Ricci again sees the thief, and again gives chase. This time the thief is on foot. Ricci pursues him into a government brothel. The madame and her help struggle to protect the thief and to throw Ricci out. "This is just too much," says one prostitute. "In the best house in Rome. Suppose the commissioner hears?" Italy is an "enlightened" society which legalizes prostitution, but cannot create jobs for men who are willing to work. Finally, Ricci succeeds in hauling the thief back on the street.

Unfortunately, Ricci is now in the neighborhood where the thief lives, and a mob soon gathers around the two men. "You can't come here accusing people," one man tells Ricci belligerently. In a society such as this one, human and Christian solidarity gives way to a solidarity in evil. Suddenly the thief has an epileptic fit; he sinks to the ground, foaming at the mouth. Here, too, De Sica's sympathy for all men seems to be manifest. The thief—despicable as he is—remains a human being, too, a poor sick wretch driven to crime out of need and frustration. Throughout *The Bicycle Thief*, the film-maker obliges the viewer to think, as well as feel, to ponder the question: What needs to be done to make this a truly human society?

In an effort to help his father, Bruno brings a policeman to the scene. But an inspection of the thief's flat yields nothing. The policeman cannot arrest the thief, nor can he offer any encouragement to Ricci. "All those people are witnesses for him," he says of the mob. Some toughs from the crowd follow Ricci and Bruno until they leave the thief's neighborhood. The search for the stolen bicycle is over.

The only way to survive in society, it would seem, is to steal. In Italian, De Sica's film is entitled *Ladri de Biciclette*, which translates as *The Bicycle Thieves*.* This is a more accurate title than the English version because the scenes at the Piazza Vittorio and the Porta Portese suggest that stealing bicycles is a way of life in Italy and that Ricci is a representative type: the victim of a theft, he is himself finally forced to steal in order to save himself. At the end, Ricci also becomes a bicycle thief.

Shot of Ricci and Bruno sitting dejectedly on a curb, opposite a sports arena. Hundreds of bicycles are parked outside, in view of Ricci, while inside the arena we can hear the crowd enjoying themselves. Ricci eyes the bicycles. Up the street, next to the door of the house, another bike rests against a wall. One can read Ricci's thoughts: "Should I steal the lone bicycle—or one from the hundreds outside the arena?" Ricci gets up, paces nervously about, struggling with himself. Suddenly he takes some change from his pocket. "Here, Bruno," he says, "take that trolley to Monte Sacro and wait for me." Bruno misses the trolley and is forced to wait for another. As a result, he sees his father steal another man's bicycle.

Because Ricci is fundamentally a good man, he bungles the theft. Unlike a professional thief, he does not use his son as a

---

* Or, literally, *The Thieves of Bicycles*.

partner. Furthermore, an experienced thief probably would
have selected one bike from the hundreds parked in front of the
arena. That way, if he was caught, he could argue that he had
made a mistake. but Ricci chooses the lone bike—and then
steals it just as its owner appears. Finally, he feels so nervous
and guilty that he bicycles poorly and is easily apprehended by
a mob. "Thief! Thief! Stop him!" shouts the owner of the
bicycle, echoing Ricci's exact words earlier in the film when *his*
bicycle was stolen. "Take him to prison," someone says. And
another strikes Ricci, knocking his hat to the ground.

Shot of Bruno, trying to reach his father, pushing his way
through the crowd. He picks up his father's hat, dusts it off,
tears rolling down his cheeks. Some men are pulling Ricci
toward a police station. Bruno runs up and takes hold of his
father's leg. Suddenly the owner of the bicycle is moved by compassion and understanding. "I don't want to make trouble," he
says. "Let's forget it." Reluctantly, the crowd frees Ricci.

The Bicycle Thief concludes with Ricci and Bruno walking
together through the crowded city. Bruno hands his father the
battered hat. Ricci can barely keep from crying; he moves forward woodenly. His son keeps gazing up at him. Close-up of
Bruno's hand reaching for that of his father—it is a sign of love,
comprehension, forgiveness; it is a symbol of equal partnership
in whatever lies ahead for the family. Still holding hands, father
and son walk through the twilight of a Sunday evening, and
disappear into the crowd. There is no bicycle, and no job . . .
but there is love, and therefore hope. "Everything sorts itself
out, except death."

The ending of *The Bicycle Thief* is surely one of the most
memorable and moving scenes in the whole of cinema.

4

Ikiru
1952

Akira Kurosawa's *Ikiru* (*To Live*)* opens with a close-up of an X-ray negative. Off-screen, we hear the voice of a narrator: "This is an X-ray of a stomach. It belongs to the man this story is about. He has cancer, but as yet he doesn't realize it." Kurosawa then cuts to a shot of Kanji Watanabe (Takashi Shimura), Chief of the Citizen's Section at City Hall, who is sitting behind a desk stacked high with papers. At the front of the office is the information desk. On the desk is a sign which reads: "THIS WINDOW IS FOR YOU. IT IS YOUR LINK WITH THE CITY HALL. WE WELCOME BOTH REQUESTS AND COMPLAINTS." Some women are complaining to Sakei (Haruo Tanaka), the clerk, about a swampy lot in their neighborhood which is a disease-breeding ground spreading sickness among their children. They suggest that a playground be erected on the spot.

Off-screen, the narrator informs us that Watanabe is the central character in the film, but that so far he is just wasting his time: "It would be difficult to say that he is really alive." When Sakei tells Watanabe about the womens' request, the hero instructs him to send them to the Public Works Section. Throughout this scene, Watanabe keeps looking at his watch—waiting for his day at the office to end. Yet he has so little time left.

* Also entitled *Living* and *Doomed.*

A girl in the office—Toyo (Miki Odagiri)—is laughing at a joke she read. But when she tells her fellow clerks the joke ("You've never had a day off? Why? Because I don't want them to discover that they don't really need me.") nobody laughs. The narrator's voice is in counterpoint to what we have just seen and heard: "Watanabe is like a dead man. In fact, he has been dead for twenty-five years. Before that he had some life in him—he even tried to work." Shot of Watanabe cleaning his seal with a sheet of paper on which is written: "A PLAN TO INCREASE OFFICE EFFICIENCY." The narrator goes on to say that Watanabe's ambition has been stifled by the bureaucracy. Although our hero keeps constantly busy, he accomplishes nothing. This is not the way to live. "But before Watanabe starts to think seriously," the narrator concludes, "his pain must increase and more time must be wasted."

Kurosawa then shows us how the women who Watanabe sent to the Public Works Section are faring. The head of that section sends the women to the Parks Section. From there they are sent to the Health Center . . . then to the Sanitation Section . . . then to the Environmental Health Section . . . and on and on through eight more departments—until the women return to the point where they began: the Citizen's Section. Nobody helps them; nobody sees their human problem. Throughout this scene, each department head gazes directly into the camera, thus forcing the audiences into an identification with the housewives. In order to shift quickly from one department to the next, Kurosawa uses wipes.

Dissolve from the office to the waiting room of a hospital. A man, who is also a patient, tells Watanabe that the doctors are not honest. When they discover cancer of the stomach, they inform you that it is only an ulcer, that an operation is unnecessary. But your stomach has a heavy feeling; you are constantly thirsty; you have gas; you have either diarrhea or you are constipated; your stool is always black. As the man recites the symptoms of stomach cancer, Watanabe keeps moving away from him—and closer to the camera. Watanabe tries to escape the truth, but as he gets closer to us, the truth is pressed in on him. We can see it in his bulging eyes, the fear working in his face. When a nurse calls Watanabe to see the doctor, Kurosawa cuts to a long shot of the protagonist. He is seen alone in the distance, his back to the camera, lost in gloomy thoughts.

Inside the doctor's office, Watanabe learns his fate. "It's just a light case of ulcers," he is told. After Watanabe leaves, the doctor informs an associate that Watanabe has no more than six months to live.

Outside Watanabe is seen walking on the street. Although he remains surrounded by people and traffic, there is no sound. Watanabe has withdrawn completely into himself; he sees and hears nothing—until a truck almost hits him. Then there is the sudden roar of a motor, and the protagonist is shocked into awareness of everything going on around him. Long shot of Watanabe, standing on the opposite curb, looking small and ineffectual. Kurosawa's use of sight and sound and silence here is brilliant.

Wipe to a shot of the exterior of Watanabe's house. It is night. Mitsuo (Nobuo Kaneko), Watanabe's son, and Kazue (Kzoko Seki), Mitsuo's wife, appear. They are discussing the possibility of buying a new house. As they open the door to their present home and walk upstairs in the dark, they decide that they could afford a new house, if they used some of Watanabe's retirement pay and savings. Kazue says: "Do you think he'll agree?" To which Mitsuo replies: "If he doesn's he'll have to live by himself. He can't take it with him, can he?" And the loving son laughs.

Mitsuo's mirth dies, however, when he discovers his father sitting in the dark in the upstairs rooms. "What's the matter?" asks Mitsuo; but Watanabe goes downstairs to his own rooms without telling his son about his condition. Obviously, he had wanted solace; however, having heard the conversation between Mitsuo and Kazue, he realizes that his son and daughter-in-law are unfeeling. He would get no comfort from them. In this scene, Kurosawa again dramatically juxtaposes sound and silence. He cuts from a shot of the couple talking on the stairs about using Watanabe's money for a new house—to a shot of Watanabe sitting alone, in complete silence, in the dark.

In his room now, Watanabe gazes at a photograph of his late wife. Close-up of the picture . . . Dissolve to a shot of a hearse, viewed through the windshield of a car behind it. Rain is falling. In the back seat of the car are Watanabe; Kiichi (Makoto Kobori), his older brother; Tatsu (Kumeko Urahe), Kiichi's wife; and Mitsuo as a child. Cut back to Watanabe's room. Upstairs Mitsuo and Kazue appear to making love. Watanabe stares thoughtfully at the ceiling—then there is another cut to a shot of a younger Watanabe, talking to his brother. Kiichi tells Watanabe to get married again; to deny himself that happiness for Mitsuo's sake would be folly. "When he grows up," Kiichi warns, "he's not going to be all that grateful. Once he gets married himself, you'll be in the way." In the flashback, Watanabe hears little Mitsuo calling him. Cut back to the present. Again Watanabe hears his son calling him. Suddenly Watanabe looks hopeful: perhaps Mitsuo has noticed something wrong with his father, perhaps he will listen as his father tells him of his cancer, his sense of a life wasted. Painfully climbing the stairs, Watanabe abruptly halts when the light goes out in his son's room—and with it his last hope of communicating with Mitsuo. Off-screen, we hear Mitsuo's voice: "Goodnight. And don't forget to lock up." Watanabe rests his forehead against a step, whispering disconsolately: "Mitsuo."

Watanabe pads downstairs again, crosses the hallway, and locks the front door. From a corner, he removes a baseball bat and fixes it against the door for added protection. Kurosawa cuts to a close-up of the bat. Sound of a baseball being struck. Cheers. Cut to a shot of Watanabe watching young Mitsuo running the bases. Before he can reach home plate, though, Mitsuo collapses. Cut to a hospital. "Be brave, Mitsuo," Watanabe says. "An appendix operation isn't anything to worry about." And Mitsuo is taken away on a stretcher.

Cut back to Watanabe, still standing in the hallway, repeating his son's name.

Another flashback. It is wartime; and Mitsuo is in uniform. The scene is a railway station, crowded with people. Shot of a sorrowful Mitsuo as his train pulls out of the station. The worried father calls his son's name: "Mitsuo . . . Mitsuo . . . Mitsuo."

Slow dissolve from the face of Mitsuo to a shot of Watanabe, standing in the hall. He has been remembering the most emotional moments he had shared with the son he loves so much—the son who now shows no evidence of love for his father. Back in his room, Watanabe climbs fearfully into bed, pulling the covers over his face. He begins to sob. Close-up of a framed letter on the wall: "MR. KANJI WATANABE IS HEREBY GIVEN RECOGNITION FOR HIS TWENTY-FIVE YEARS OF DEVOTED SERVICE." The ironies in *Ikiru* remind one of Tolstoy's great novelette, *The Death of Ivan Ilych*, which Kurosawa most certainly must have read.[1]

This is the end of the first section in the structure of *Ikiru.* We have been introduced to Watanabe; he knows that he is going to die; he sees that he has wasted his life for almost thirty years at a stultifying job; and, furthermore, he realizes that he has sacrificed in vain for his beloved son, Mitsuo. In the following three sections of the film Watanabe will seek to find a way of enjoying the little time he has left, to make what remains of his life count for something.

We next encounter Watanabe at a bar. He has not been to work for five days; and he has withdrawn fifty thousand yen from the bank. It is clear that Watanabe's first attempt to make his last days on earth significant will be in the direction of hedonism. In short, he will seek sense pleasure. Unfortunately, however, Watanabe discovers that his condition makes having fun difficult. Because of his stomach cancer, he can drink only so much before vomiting. Moreover, the alcohol does not even taste good to him.

In the bar, Watanabe encounters a sympathetic young writer (Yunosuke Ito), who agrees to show the dying man a good time. "Look, keep your money," the writer says. "You'll be my guest tonight." The writer explains that, even though

A memorable close-up from *Ikiru*. Watanabe (Takashi Shimura) weeps as he contemplates his death.

death is terrible, a man may discover meaning in tragedy. Life looks much more beautiful to one who is about to leave it than to one who is safe and healthy. "Some die," the young man tells Watanabe, "without ever once knowing what life is really like." The writer admires what Dylan Thomas calls that "rage against the dying of the light." Calling himself Watanabe's "Mephistopheles"—"but a good one," he adds, "one who won't ask to be paid"—the writer, who even finds a black dog, leads the old man out into the darkness.*

The writer takes Watanabe to a huge beer hall, where a band is playing. A girl steals Watanabe's hat, but the writer tells the dying man not to worry about it. "We're going to buy you a new hat to say goodbye to your old life with," he says. Shot of Watanabe and the writer in another bar. The old man has his new hat, now, and he guards it as though it were a priceless treasure. "He's God," the writer remarks of Watanabe to the woman who owns the place. "And he's carrying this cross called cancer." Wipe to a cabaret. A piano player asks for requests. Watanabe suggests "Life Is So Short," an old popular love song. While the pianist plays, Watanabe sings:

> Life is so short,
> Fall in love, dear maiden,
> While your lips are still red;
> Before you can no longer love—
> For there will be no tomorrow.

As Watanabe sings mournfully, Kurosawa's camera tracks slowly around him in close. The old man is weeping. People move away from him, and when the song ends there is utter silence.

Cut to a striptease dancer on a platform, wriggling in a circle of light, men staring up at her. We see the girl reach for a button on her costume. Cut to the floor as her skirt drops off. Cut to the drunken faces of Watanabe and the writer. The latter says: "That isn't art. A striptease isn't art—it's too direct. It's more direct than art." Watanabe's eyes are bulging

---

* The writer's allusions, of course, are to Goethe's *Faust*.

out of his head—the girl is obviously naked now—and the dying man moans with desire. As Kurosawa shoots this scene it is, by the writer's definition, art—because we never see the stripper naked. The fact of her nakedness is presented to us indirectly.

Next we find Watanabe and the writer in a dance hall. The floor is packed. Watanabe is dancing with a girl who is clearly bored with the proceedings . . . Shot of Watanabe, the writer, and two girls in a car. One girl is counting a roll of bills, the other is removing false eyelashes. Suddenly Watanabe has to vomit. *La dolce vita* is not so sweet . . . And thus ends the second section in the structure of *Ikiru*.

The third section of Kurosawa's masterpiece commences when Watanabe, the morning following his night with the writer, meets Toyo on the street. The office girl has a new job and she needs Watanabe's seal on her papers. Watanabe, who is not going to work, takes the girl home, where he has his seal. In his room, he speaks honestly about the emptiness he had experienced in almost thirty years on the job. "I can't remember one day, one thing I did," he says. "All I know is that I was always busy, and always bored." Upstairs Mitsuo and Kazue speculate as to whether Watanabe is having an affair with Toyo. Downstairs again, the old man notices that Toyo has holes in her stockings. It is obvious that Watanabe is cheered by the girl's presence, by her health and vitality. Consequently, he takes her to a shop where he buys her a new pair of stockings; then he goes with her to a tearoom. While there, she amuses Watanabe by telling him the nicknames she made up for everyone in the office—Mr. Sea-Slug, Mr. Drain-Cover, Mr. Fly-Paper, Mr. Menu, Mr. Jello . . . She remains reluctant, though, to tell Watanabe her nickname for him. He insists. "I wouldn't mind," he says. "I'd like it if you made it up." Finally, she tells him: Mr. Mummy. They both laugh.

Shots of Watanabe and Toyo playing a pinball machine; ice skating; eating noodles; devouring ice cream; Toyo watching a film, Watanabe asleep beside her; the two of them eating dinner. Once again, Kurosawa manages the transitions through the use of wipes.

In the restaurant, Watanabe tells Toyo that he became a "mummy" for Mitsuo's sake and now sees that it was a terrible error. But Toyo will not let Watanabe shift the responsibility for his life from himself to his son. "Your son," she says, "didn't ask you to become a mummy." Watanabe smiles when Toyo reminds him that he still loves Mitsuo . . . But when Watanabe goes home to tell his son about the cancer, Mitsuo cuts him short because he thinks that his father wants to talk about the "affair" with Toyo. Hurt again, Watanabe goes back to his room.

Fade in on Watanabe's empty chair at City Hall. The clerks in the office are discussing the "mummy." Off-screen, we hear the voice of the narrator, who informs us that Watanabe's co-workers all believe that he is conducting himself stupidly. "Yet," concludes the narrator, "to Watanabe, his behavior represents the most meaningful actions of his whole life."

Shot of Watanabe talking to Toyo outside the toy factory where she now works. Watanabe is begging the girl to see him again that night, but she tells him that she is tired after working all day and weary of going out with him every night. Finally, however, she agrees.

Wipe to the following scene: a coffeehouse. Watanabe and Toyo are seated at a table; nearby is a group of boys and girls, celebrating someone's birthday. Kurosawa plays off the joy of the children against the gloom of Watanabe and Toyo. But the film-maker is also, very skillfully, preparing the viewer for the final section in the film structure. Toyo tells Watanabe that she is bored. "Why do you want to be with me all the time?" she asks. Watanabe admits (to Toyo's relief) that he does not love her. At first, the old man has difficulty explaining his feelings. Finally, he tells her that he has cancer. When he received his death sentence, he suddenly felt drawn to her. Just to gaze at her made him feel good. He responded to her kindness, to her youth and health. But mainly, Watanabe says, he remains envious of her vitality. "You are so full of life," he says. "If only I could be like you for one day before I die. Oh, I want to do something." And Watanabe asks Toyo to tell him how he should live out his final days.

Shot of Toyo (Miki Odagiri) and Watanabe in a coffeehouse. Watanabe asks the young woman how he should live until he dies. Toyo tells him to spend his final days making others happy.

Toyo removes a toy rabbit from her pocket. All I do she tells him, is eat and work and make toys. "I feel as if I were friends with all the children in Japan now," she says. "Mr. Watanabe, why don't you do something like that, too?" At first, the dying man is nonplussed. Then, with sudden determination, Watanabe seizes the toy rabbit and bolts away from the table. "I *can* do something," he announces, "if I really want to!" Watanabe exits hurriedly, past the boys and girls shouting "Happy Birthday!" Fade out . . .

Fade in to a shot of Watanabe's office. The clerks are speculating that the dying man will soon resign, but when the cancer victim unexpectedly appears, he upsets their calculations. He searches his desk until he finds a document on which is written: "PETITION FOR RECLAIMING DRAINAGE AREA—KUROE-CHO WOMEN'S ASSOCIATION." Attached to the document is a notice: "This petition is to be forwarded to the Public Works Section." Tearing off the notice, Watanabe says that unless everyone cooperates nothing will ever be done. And out he goes, petition in hand, to make an inspection of the land and to prepare a report. On the sound track is heard "Happy Birthday."

Thus ends the third section in the structure of *Ikiru*. In the first section, Watanabe had learned that he was going to die but that, in truth, all his years had been a kind of death-in-life. He had come to realize that he had loved Mitsuo not wisely but too well. In the second section, the Mephistophelian writer had tried to introduce Watanabe to the sensual pleasures of life: but the alcohol made the old man vomit and the whores did not satisfy his deepest hunger. In the third section, Watanabe tries to live his youth again in company with Toyo—but you can't go home again. The writer had referred to Watanabe as a God; that is, as a Christ, carrying a cross in the form of cancer. In the final section of *Ikiru*, Watanabe moves beyond familial love, sexual love, and regressive love; he learns what it means "to live." For Kurosawa, altruistic or benevolent love is the answer to the problem of human existence. Like Christ, Watanabe will sacrifice himself for others—he will spend his last days in the service of others. He will turn a swampy lot into a playground for children.

The final section of *Ikiru* begins with a shot of a photograph of Watanabe on a funeral altar. Off-screen, the narrator tells us that five months after our hero decided to help the children he died. The funeral altar is in Watanabe's room; and the office personnel are all present, as are the mayor (Nubuo Nakamura) and Watanabe's family. Everyone is drinking saké and kneeling on cushions arranged on both sides of the altar. Some reporters arrive to question the mayor about the playground. It seems the mayor and the Parks Section are claiming responsibility for the project, the reporters observe, when in reality Watanabe deserves the credit. According to the reporters, Watanabe was not even mentioned by the mayor at the dedication ceremony, though he was given a seat at the back. We also learn that the people know the truth about the matter, and that Watanabe died one cold night in the playground built by his efforts.

A group of women from Kuroe-Cho enter, some of whom we met at the beginning of the film. They have come to pay their respects. Tears in their eyes, they bow before Watanabe's photograph. Incense is burned. The mayor and his lackeys appear uncomfortable. Then, without a word, the women leave.

After the mayor also departs, a man from the Parks Section claims sole credit for the playground. Another man says no one built the park—it just happened. The people present speculate as to whether Watanabe knew he had cancer, or whether he had kept a mistress . . . Kurosawa cuts to a shot of Watanabe walking in the rain, gazing at the spot where the playground will be . . . Cut back to the funeral party, where the small-minded discussion of the protagonist continues. The Parks Clerk says that his chief resented Watanabe . . . Cut to the past again. Here we see Watanabe putting pressure on the Chief of Parks. "The conditions there are terrible," Watanabe says; to which the bureaucrat replies: "But it isn't as easy as you make out" . . . Cut back to the funeral, where the Parks Clerk observes: "Mr. Watanabe just stayed there until the boss consented." Then Kurosawa repeats the process: we see Watanabe taking the petition through other departments, succeeding where, at the beginning of the film, the women alone had failed. Interspersed among these flashbacks are shots of the funeral party commenting on Watanabe's progress in the present. We even see Watanabe in the mayor's office, and how the mayor had resisted the idea—until the dying man just wore the official down by his persistence.

Cut to the past. Shot of a clerk named Ono (Kamatari Fujiwara) accompanying Watanabe down the steps of City Hall. "The way they treat you," Ono says. "It should make you angry to be insulted this way." But Watanabe only replies: "I don't have time to be angry with anyone." Then we see Watanabe and Ono crossing a bridge at dusk above the park site. Watanabe remarks: "How lovely. For thirty years I have never gazed at a sunset—and now it's too late." There is no sentimentality in this. As a member of the funeral party—Kimura (Shinichi Himori)—says at one point in defense of the hero: "If you can't try to understand a man like Watanabe without being thought sentimental, then the world is a dark place indeed." The funeral party finally agree that Watanabe had known he was going to die. They realize that they would all do the same as he had done if they had terminal cancer. But since they will all die eventually, either of cancer or of something else, why don't they live as Watanabe lived *now?* As an excuse, they blame their lethargy on the bureaucracy. "Why," says one clerk, "to get permission for a new garbage can you have to fill out enough papers to fill up the garbage can." The men begin to cry.

Suddenly the maid enters, carrying Watanabe's hat, which is battered and filthy. A policeman, who also enters, had found it in the park. He too wants to pay his respects. The policeman tells them that he saw Watanabe sitting on a swing in the park on the night he died. Watanabe looked happy.

Cut to the park. Long shot of Watanabe, seen through the bars of a junglegym, seated on a swing. It is snowing. The camera moves forward slowly, tracking past the junglegym, allowing us a side view of Watanabe through the bars. Presently the camera circles and positions itself directly in front of Watanabe. He is singing:

> *Life is so short,*
> *Fall in love, dear maiden,*
> *While your lips are still red;*
> *Before you can no longer love—*
> *For there will be no tomorrow.*

Cut back to Watanabe's funeral. The clerks assembled there, all of them drunk now, vow that Watanabe's death shall not have been in vain. Henceforth, they will show his spirit in getting things done at the office. Fade out . . .

Fade in to a shot of City Hall. A new man—Ono—has taken Watanabe's place as department head of the Citizen's Section. Sakei informs him that the sewage water has over-flowed in a certain district. The new department head says: "Well, send them to the Public Works Section." As Sakei repeats this direction to someone at the front of the office, Kurosawa focuses on Kimura. The camera shoots him over a pile of papers stacked on his desk—his humanity is obliterated by useless data, memos, statistical baggage.

Ikiru ends with a scene showing the clerk Kimura walking across the same bridge Ono had crossed earlier with Watanabe. It was the scene in which the dying man had stopped to admire a sunset for the first time in years. Again, it is sunset. And Kimura stops to admire it. Down below, in the park, children are playing. Shot, through the bars of the junglegym, of a child on a swing. A mother calls her son. He goes to her. Shot of the empty swing, moving slowly. Off-screen, we hear again the song "Life Is So Short," this time played hauntingly on a flute. Kimura walks off . . .*

---

* "Occasionally, I think of my death," Kurosawa has said. "Then I think, how could I ever bear to take a final breath, while living a life like this. How could I leave it? There is, I feel, so much more for me to do—I keep feeling I have lived so little yet. Then I become thoughtful, but not sad. It was from such a feeling that *Ikiru* arose."[2]

5

La Strada
1954

Since Federico Fellini was a scriptwriter for a number of neo-realist directors before making pictures himself, his films reveal traces of the neo-realist technique. Location shooting, the use of nonprofessionals in the cast, close attention to physical details—all this is reminiscent of De Sica's *The Bicycle Thief*. However, the stark "objective" style—that fidelity to external appearances—which distinguishes the cinema of the neo-realist directors is not the dominant feature of Fellini's work.

In his early films, Fellini strikes a balance between objectivism and subjectivism.* His argument with the neo-realists is that their theoretical and practical approach remains one-sided, inasmuch as they insist that films should explore social reality alone. It is Fellini's conviction that the film-maker has the freedom to present any kind of reality—social, psychological, spiritual. Critics have had great difficulty in their attempts to label Fellini's style. "Poetic cinema," "poetic neo-realism," "surreal expressionism" are favorite tags. Fellini himself has often been called a "romantic," a "baroque fantasist," an "expressionist," an "impressionist." The art of Fellini remains so rich, so various, that it can sustain any number of interpretations. Consequently, there is some cor-

Author's Note: Much of the material in this chapter appeared previously in my *Fellini the Artist*, copyright © 1976 by Frederick Ungar Publishing Co., Inc.

* *La Strada* is one of Fellini's early films. In his later films—starting with *8½* (1963)—Fellini's work becomes much more subjective.

respondence between his films and the definitions cited, just as there is some correspondence between Fellini the artist and the terms in which he has been described. One could make a good case for Fellini's art as being "romantic." There is in it a love of mystery; an emphasis on aspiration, wonder, feeling, personality, the inner world, the infinite; an extensive use of symbols and myths; a belief that nature is alive with spirits, or *a* spirit; that nature, since it is part of God, can be a revelation of the truth. Basically, Fellini's art represents a fusion of the real and the ideal—life as it is, and life as it ought to be.

Fellini possesses a vivid cinematic imagination. Unlike many directors, though, he delights the eye without recourse to visual clichés. He normally resists the temptation to exploit the large number of techniques available to anyone working in the medium—techniques that not infrequently substituted for emotion and thought and personal vision; in other words, techniques that are offered up in place of art. Fellini tends to eschew freeze frames, zoom shots, fast motion, slow motion, wipes, superimpositions, and swishpans. If one technique can be said to recur in Fellini's pictures, it is the moving camera. Since his world remains open and multiple, this procedure seems best suited to convey the twin ideas of spaciousness and manifoldness. Nevertheless, what we call "Felliniesque" cannot be defined in terms of a single technique that any run-of-the-mill director might duplicate; instead, it is made up of various elements that comprise the film-maker's "signature."

The key features of Fellini's style include a circus-like atmosphere; processions; theatrical and vaudevillian performances; seriocomic structure; a fusion of stylization and realism, empty piazzas; the road and the sea as symbolic landscapes; the alternation of noisy scenes and quiet scenes, night scenes and day scenes, scenes of estrangement and scenes of recognition; a nostalgia for childhood innocence, moral purity, sanctity. Redemption is probably Fellini's great theme—a theme which can be traced to his Roman Catholic background. The procession as ritual, the juxtaposition of contrasting scenes, the longing for goodness—these elements, as well as some others, derive whole or in part from Fellini's religious upbringing. The film-maker's irony is balanced by humor, his bitterness by sentiment, his pessimism by optimism.

As Proust contended, style is basically a matter not of technique but of vision.

La Strada (*The Road*) opens by the sea. In the pale sunlight children shout across the dunes to Gelsomina (Guilietta Masina), telling her to come home. Zampanò (Anthony Quinn), an itinerant strongman, wants to buy Gelsomina for 10,000 lire so that she can help him in his act. Once before the impoverished mother had sold a daughter to Zampanò, but that girl died on the road; now destitution again forces the woman to surrender a child, perhaps to the same fate as the previous one. From the start, Fellini visually contrasts the two main characters of his film: Gelsomina—blonde, diminutive, pixy-faced, humble in bearing; Zampanò—dark, huge, glowering, arrogant in demeanor. On one level, *La Strada* is a fable about Beauty and the Beast; in this case, however, Gelsomina's beauty is interior, not exterior, and it is Beauty who loves the Beast, not the other way round—at least for most of the picture. Before leaving the place of her birth, Gelsomina turns and kneels in the direction of the sea, in a silent farewell communion with those waters which throughout the film are identified with her. Revealing his usual sullen expression, the strongman watches the simple-minded girl on her knees. Afterward Gelsomina climbs in the back of Zampanò's motorcycle-driven trailer and the two depart—dust rising from the road, the girl crying and waving goodbye—on what is to become a spiritual odyssey for both of them.

Zampanò's main act consists of breaking an iron chain with the muscles of his chest, a performance which impresses not only the country people along the road but also Gelsomina. Over and over in the course of the picture, Zampanò utters the same words ("Sensitive souls are advised not to look. In Milan, Ettore Montagna lost his sight through this trick, since there is an enormous strain on the optic nerve . . ."), struts in a circle—

Fellini has said: "Faces are more important to me than anything else." Here we see a close-up of Gelsomina (Giulietta Masina)—perhaps the most haunting face in all of Fellini's films—in *La Strada*.

stomach in, chest out—waving his chain in the air, prior to bursting its links by inflating his lungs. The repetition of this performance underlines Zampanò's monotonous, self-enclosed manner of existence. He is an animal, and he treats other people as if they were animals. On their first evening together, Gelsomina cooks soup that is so bad even she can't eat it; although Zampanò devours the soup—as he devours everything—he still calls it "slop for pigs." At the beginning of the film, Zampanò assures Gelsomina's mother that he "can even teach a dog to perform." Now he proceeds to teach Gelsomina. Her job is to announce his act by intoning: "Zam-pan-ò is here!," followed by drumbeats as the chain is broken. Unfortunately, Gelsomina is not a fast learner. We laugh at Zampanò's attempts to make the girl understand the simple requirements of her role, but when the lout proceeds to strike Gelsomina on the leg with a switch in order to make her concentrate, the laughter dies. What starts as a kind of Abbott and Costello vaudeville turn ends by becoming something far from comedy. Just as Fellini juxtaposes beauty and bestiality, just so he alternates gaiety and sadness, the complex structure of his film moving from the serio-comic (up to about the middle of the picture) to the serious (there are few laughs in the second half of *La Strada*).

Fellini does not indulge in fancy camera work or bizarre compositions. Whenever he moves his camera, the movement is well-motivated in terms of mood, action, and theme. For example, on their first night together Zampanò tells Gelsomina to sleep with him in the trailer. She wants to sleep outside. He repeats his order. The camera-eye has been recording the scene impassively in front of the motorcycle. The characters step out of sight and start around to the back of the trailer. Slowly, the camera glides forward, makes a turn to the left, and gazes downward at the mattress. Zampanò pushes Gelsomina roughly inside the trailer and closes the flap on the tarpaulin, causing the screen to go dark. This incident remains one of the few times in the film when the viewer becomes aware of the camera. Since Gelsomina is frightened, the camera seems hesitant, unwilling to look at what is to follow; the camera's eventual intrusion—with its serpentine downward motion—is both intimate and faintly ominous.

The structure of *La Strada* can be described as episodic. As Zampanò and Gelsomina journey from town to town, characters are introduced and then seen no more—which is life-like but unlike plotted films where characters who appear at the beginning must also function in the middle and reappear at the end. Fellini's classic is unified thematically. A scene which at first might strike the viewer as a digression later reveals its relevance to the overall design. Although Fellini structures his action vertically by concentrating on character development and idea, he also provides horizontal movement or story interest, for the viewer wants to know what will happen next. Indeed, it is almost impossible to separate vertical and horizontal movement, or character exploration and story, so closely has Fellini woven together the various elements of his picture.

Like all his films, Fellini's *La Strada* is open in structure, thus reflecting his view of life as a mystery filled with unpredictable possibilities. Throughout the movie, Fellini alternates a day scene with a night scene, a rhythmic pattern which finds its musical parallel in Nino Rota's famous recurrent tune. As a scene enacted in bleak, sometimes cold sunlight gives way to a scene involving an empty street or a market place at night, the music comes and goes throughout; hence, the score not only augments the happy-sad thematic approach but also functions as a structural device for unifying the whole. The result is an exquisite blending of realism (the location shooting, the numerous nonprofessionals in the cast, the holes in Zampanò's sweater and pants) and a kind of "poetic," "lyrical" expressionism or surrealism (the numerous symbols, the fable-like quality of the action, the stylized conception of the three chief personages).

Fellini rarely puts his meaning into words; when he does, as we shall see, it is generally because certain ideas cannot be expressed in any other way. However, through his manner of linking scenes, Fellini not only gives his form continuity but he also supplies nonverbal commentary. After the screen goes black in the trailer, for instance, there is a scene in which Gelsomina wakes up in the night and begins to cry. Zampanò—his sexual appetite satisfied—is sleeping. Even though she has been taken against her will, even though her body has been used without respect for her person, Gelsomina stops weeping momentarily to gaze fondly at the unconscious male who has somehow, in spite of himself, aroused her love and inspired her hope. But the next shot makes clear how little Gelsomina can really expect from the future. It is the following day; and on the screen we see the strongman with a chain stretched across his chest: food, drink, breaking the chain, sex, sleep—Zampanò knows only these physical activities and needs.

Evening. The couple visit a cafe. Zampanò is in his customary surly mood, but Gelsomina is delighted with the experience. When Zampanò, before eating, pokes a toothpick around in his mouth, Gelsomina imitates her hero; likewise she mops her plate greedily with a crust of bread as he does, and she even tries to drink as much wine as the strongman. To no avail. Zampanò ignores the clownish little creature who shares his mean existence, constantly foiling her attempts at intimacy with disdain:

> *Gelsomina:* Where do you come from?
> *Zampanò:* From my part of the country.
> *Gelsomina:* Where were you born?
> *Zampanò:* (Sneering) In my father's house.

Drunk now, Zampanò notices a buxom, red-headed woman across the room and calls her over to their table. During this scene the strongman shows off his muscles and makes the woman laugh, treating her in a way he never treats the faithful wretch who assists him in his act. All the same, Gelsomina fails to understand what is happening, fails to grasp the fact that Zampanò intends to spend the night with the fat redhead; so she naïvely laughs along with the other two, with no trace of jealousy apparent on her innocent countenance. However, in order for the viewer to see the scene from Gelsomina's perspective—or, rather, to see what Gelsomina would see if she had eyes to see—Fellini shoots the action partly from her viewpoint. The camera-eye does not actually "see" what Gelsomina sees; nevertheless, although her skull remains visible on the screen, the shot is clearly angled from her point of view, since the camera is situated just in back of her head. Outside the cafe, Zampanò helps the other woman onto his motorcycle and instructs the confused Gelsomina to wait behind for him. "But where are you going?" she cries. There is no reply . . . only the sound of the motorcycle fading into the night.

Dissolve. It is dark and quiet . . . and Gelsomina is still waiting for Zampanò. As she morosely sits at the curb, a horse suddenly emerges and noisily *clipclops* past. The appearance of this stray, riderless animal has occasioned much comment. John Russell Taylor, for example, observes: "the effect is positively surrealistic: totally arbitrary, yet giving an instant visual reinforcement to the mood of the scene. The lost horse might well be a figment of Gelsomina's imagination, an image of her own state. But it is also a real horse, and its appearance here at this time is not impossible, only mildly peculiar."[1] Is Fellini "saying" that Gelsomina is like a horse without a rider? Certainly the strongman treats her no better than he would a horse. In Fellini's *La Dolce Vita* (1959), Marcello—who has some traits in common with Zampanò—rides on the back of a woman who is down on all fours. During a later scene in *La Strada*, Zampanò says to a woman with whom he has sexual relations: "Do you always eat standing up like a horse?" In the same scene, Gelsomina worries about a sick horse; and near the end of the film, just before he deserts her, Zampanò tells Gelsomina that she too is sick. The sequence in which Zampanò leaves Gelsomina to wait for him while he sleeps with the redhead (who, not surprisingly, robs him of all his money), together with the shot of the riderless horse, not only rehearses the final desertion but also suggests another scene in *La Dolce Vita*. In the later film, Emma accuses Marcello of not being able to love; he concurs—but argues that he does not want to spend his entire life caring for her. After slapping Emma, Marcello

pushes her out of his car. Hurt and angry, she tells him:
"You've lost the only thing of value in life—a woman who
really loves you. Someday you'll be old. There'll be no more
women. And you'll die alone like a dog!" Later Marcello comes
back for Emma—who, like Gelsomina, has waited for her man
on the road—but the couple have no future together. The situation is the same in *La Strada*.

Morning. A child sits on the curb beside the petulant
Gelsomina. Also beside her is a plate of food left by a com-
passionate woman, but Gelsomina has left it untouched. When
the woman returns, she informs Gelsomina that a man is sleeping in a field down the road, near a moto-trailer. Happily,
Gelsomina returns to her brutal master. Dancing lightly across
the desolate landscape, she suddenly pauses before a single bare
tree. A child passes, watching her. With arms outstretched, a
smile lighting up her small puffy face, Gelsomina imitates the
tree. A boy approaches. "The dog died in there," he informs
her, pointing to an area beyond a fence. Standing before the
dog's burial ground, Gelsomina looks inside, wonderment
evident in her expression. She listens for something. For what?
Gelsomina communicates intuitively with the sea, with trees,
even with the spirit of a dead dog. She is witness to a reality
beyond the one which can be seen or touched. Yet, at the same
time, she is very much a part of that natural world whose inner
being she mysteriously apprehends. Because she longs to see the
various manifestations of the Good—be it love or a tree—take
root and grow, she plants tomato seeds by the side of the road,
even though Zampanò plans to move on again. To her
astonished question: "Are we leaving already?" Zampanò con-
temptuously replies: "Think we're going to stay here 'till your
tomatoes come up? *Tomatoes!*" The brute's lack of understanding remains abysmal.

Fade in to a shot of an open area where a wedding celebra-
tion is taking place. On one side there is a long banquet table
with happy people eating and drinking; on the other side Zampanò and Gelsomina are performing. Seated on the ground,
Zampanò is beating a drum, while Gelsomina, wearing a

bowler hat and clown's makeup, goes through a simple dance number. Except for some children watching Gelsomina in the background, the act goes largely unnoticed. A man offers Gelsomina a glass of wine; she takes a sip, then unselfishly passes it along to Zampanò. During this scene, Fellini again moves his camera to advantage. There is a long tracking shot the length of the banquet table: faces of happy celebrants, a priest eating, wine glasses raised, confetti, the bride and groom; cut to a momentary shot of other celebrants again—followed by a shot of Gelsomina and Zampanò, set apart from the others. The visual juxtaposition of the bride and Gelsomina speaks for itself; the contrast between the boisterous fun along the table and the dreary routine of Gelsomina's life with Zampanò requires no verbal underlining. It tells us something about Fellini's tact that he does not starkly play off the image of the bride with a shot of Gelsomina, but instead separates the two images with a brief shot of a few guests in order to convey the relational nature of his editing in a more subtle manner.

A woman calls Zampanò and Gelsomina to the farmhouse to eat. The children who have been watching Gelsomina perform intercept her, however, and lead her around to the side of the building and up a narrow flight of stairs. Skillfully employing a subjective camera, Fellini takes the audience via identification with Gelsomina's field of vision along a series of dimly lighted corridors. Shot of a tiny boy in a black cape; he looks made up to resemble a priest, or perhaps a magician. An air of the uncanny suffuses the scene. And when Gelsomina is led into a dark room the subjective camera intensifies the viewer's sensation of entering the unknown. In a large bed, propped up on pillows, sits an idiot boy named Oswaldo; he stares at Gelsomina with a frightened gaze. The children want her to amuse the lad. Yet Gelsomina's imitation of a bird only seems to increase Oswaldo's fright. Tentatively, she steps closer to the bed, exchanging a silent, wide-eyed gaze with the strange creature opposite her. All at once, a nun enters the room and angrily chases Gelsomina and the children away.

The scene involving Oswaldo is based on an experience

from Fellini's boyhood when he visited his grandmother in Gambettola. The film-maker has provided his own interpretation of the episode:

> I probably used it to give Gelsomina an exact awareness of solitude. There is a feast at the farm and Gelsomina, who ultimately is a creature who likes to be in the company of other people, and who wants to take part in the singing and in the general gaiety, is led off by this host of children who, shouting, take her to see the sick boy. The apparition of this creature who is so isolated, and a prey to delirium—and who thus has an extremely mysterious dimension—it seems to me that uniting him in a close-up with Gelsomina, who comes right next to him and who looks at him with curiosity, underlines with rather great suggestive power Gelsomina's own solitude.[2]

While Gelsomina has been making her discovery of solitude, Zampanò has been making the acquaintance of the woman who called the performers to eat. Positioned outside the kitchen, Zampanò and the woman are discoursing on sex and swallowing their food ravenously. (This is the woman to whom Zampanò remarks: "Do you always eat standing up like a horse?"). The woman has buried two husbands; she would now like to give Zampanò some suits and a hat left behind by her first mate, in exchange for some lovemaking on the part of the strongman. Gelsomina joins them; but when she tries to explain to Zampanò about Oswaldo, the brute ignores her. As he so often does, Fellini here makes use of juxtaposition. Gelsomina's encounter with the mysterious boy represents a discovery of her own loneliness: she yearns for Zampanò to recognize her as a person, to genuinely share his life with her—not merely to exploit her in his act and to use her body for sexual purposes. To be sure, the farm woman also knows solitude; like Zampanò, however, all she thinks about are her physical needs (stuffing her face with macaroni, for example, she refers to sex as a "sweet"). Finally, Zampanò dissappears with the woman, once more leaving Gelsomina to wait for him . . .

Dusk. The wedding party is over, except for one last couple, still dancing to the accompaniment of a remaining musician. A lone tree is prominent in the composition. Next Fellini reveals Gelsomina, from within a barn, studying the scene we have just witnessed. The tree outside reminds the viewer of the single tree which Gelsomina imitated in the previous sequence; later in the film, as Zampanò's moto-trailer journeys down a road, a bare tree again appears in the distance. Thematically, the lonely Gelsomina and the motif of a bare, isolated tree are what literary critic Kenneth Burke calls "equations." Humming the tune which is likewise associated with her throughout the film, Gelsomina asks Zampanò to teach her to play it on the trumpet. The strongman, however, is absorbed in trying on his newly acquired clothes; he makes no reply. Preening himself in a pin-striped suit and snapping down the brim on his fedora, Zampanò mutters scornfully, *"Women!"* just as he had previously muttered, *"Tomatoes!"* Angry at Zampanò's refusal to respond, Gelsomina strides back and forth across the barn—until she falls into a deep hole. Zampanò is amused but Gelsomina obstinately decides to spend the night below. Although the scene is played in a seriocomic fashion, Gelsomina's confinement in the ground represents one of numerous ways Fellini foreshadows her death.

Dissolve to morning. As though reborn, Gelsomina removes the clothes Zampanò had given her and proceeds to set off in her original garb on a journey by herself, thus leaving the sleeping brute (in the clothes the farm woman has given *him*) to seek another slave for his act . . . Shot of Gelsomina sitting by the side of the road, examining a bug with curiosity and wonder. Suddenly three musicians appear out of nowhere, marching along in single file, and Gelsomina, stirred by their spirited playing, jumps up and follows them . . . The procession involving the three musicians and Gelsomina gives way in the next scene to a conventional religious procession. Shots of a bishop coldly and mechanically blessing the enthusiastic faithful. Shots of the crowd. Shots of a huge cross and other traditional symbols. When Fellini shows us Gelsomina, who is thrilled by the event, he keeps his camera up close and moving with her; hence we tend to identify with Gelsomina, we experience her own emotions, we too are caught up in the excitement. In one long shot Fellini reveals the procession on the right-hand side of the screen, while on the left-hand side he presents a sign reading: BAR. The film-maker is fond of such polarities (consider, for example, the opening of *La Dolce Vita*, in which the statue of Christ suspended from a helicopter remains juxtaposed to bikini-clad girls sunbathing on a rooftop). In *La Strada* "procession" equals "quest for love and spiritual meaning" (the Gelsomina motif), whereas "BAR" equals "drunkenness, brawling, and casual sex" (the Zampanò motif). When Gelsomina and the other members of the procession enter a church, Fellini again uses a subjective camera, a visual strategy which calls to mind the experience at the farm when the children led Gelsomina into the mysterious room of Oswaldo. By using the same kind of camera technique in both scenes, Fellini links up the two events thematically.

But if Gelsomina learned something about solitude from her meeting with Oswaldo, she is not blessed with a similar dis-covery upon stepping inside the church. From a low-angle sub-jective shot of the church interior, Fellini dissolves to the next scene: a shot of Il Matto (Richard Basehart), or The Fool, on a tightrope above a piazza at night. "In a moment," a woman working with the acrobat says into a loudspeaker, "Il Matto will perform the most dangerous of his stunts. Sitting forty meters above the earth, he will eat a dish of spaghetti." Gelsomina looks up to God, but the answer to her prayer comes in the next scene when she again looks up—this time at Il Matto. Fellini has said that The Fool is "Jesus." And not surprisingly, critics have managed to ferret out the "Christ symbolism": suspended high overhead, the acrobat is equipped with angel's wings; in one scene, he rides a donkey, just as Jesus did on Palm Sunday; also like Christ, The Fool predicts his own death; and when Zampanò finally kills the equilibrist, he drags the corpse over the ground in a cruciform manner. In

74

religious art, Christ is never depicted with wings; still, one could argue that both Christ and angels are associated in a spiritual way. Unlike Christ, The Fool does not willingly sacrifice his life for Zampanò; Gelsomina performs that function, though partly as a result of what she learns from The Fool. Christ provoked his executioners, and Il Matto torments Zampanò; however, Christ was motivated by the desire to show men how to live a more authentic existence, whereas The Fool taunts Zampanò out of irrational malice. The "Christ symbolism" is present, then, but it appears in an ambiguous way. Near the end of the film, just before his recognition scene, Zampanò shouts: *"Ho bisogno di nessuno"*; but twice in the picture, Il Matto repeats the same words to Gelsomina: "I don't need anyone." In short, Fellini avoids a too neat symbolic dovetailing of Christ and Il Matto. Yet, as noted, the link *is* there. Fellini suggests that Jesus must be sought outside the Church, that in the present age Christ appears to men under different manifestations, even in the guise of a circus performer. ("Today, we are finished with the Christian myth, and await a new one," Fellini observed in 1970. "Maybe the myth is LSD? And the new Christ comes to us in this form?") As suggested previously, Il Matto is associated with another fool—namely Oswaldo—in that Gelsomina learns something from both of them. Of course, Gelsomina is a simpleton herself; and Il Matto is not really a fool—he merely plays the part of one. Furthermore, there is a sense in which Fellini's method of representation remains solidly traditional: for those who have truly sought to live according to the teachings of Christ—that is to say, those who have taken seriously such injunctions as: "Thou shalt love thy neighbor as thyself"—have frequently been called "fools for Christ." And Fellini has always had a weakness for such people. Clearly, then, the symbolism involving Il Matto in *La Strada* cannot be reduced to a single pat explanation.

Following the scene in which Gelsomina sees The Fool for the first time, Fellini shows us the gloomy square after the performers and the crowd have gone. Scraps of paper blow fitfully in front of an ancient fountain; looking feverish,

Gelsomina pats a few drops of water on her brow. Some men, who are huddled nearby in the darkness, watch her; one of them grabs at her, muttering the word "balmy," but she slips away from him. Suddenly Zampanò appears. Descending from his motorcycle, he slaps Gelsomina several times and forces her into the back of his trailer. Then, gazing belligerently at the onlookers, he asks: "Any objections?" No reply. "That's what I thought," he growls. And off he goes, taking Gelsomina with him once more . . .

Daylight. Zampanò and Gelsomina are discovered in the act of signing up for work in Colombaioni's Circus. Here Gelsomina encounters The Fool again, for he too is now a member of the troupe. Gelsomina is delighted with the acrobat (who plays a tiny violin with a cigarette fastened to its end) but she is dismayed by his habit of teasing the vicious Zampanò. When Gelsomina asks the strongman what the fool has against him, he replies: "I don't know." Nor can his tormentor offer a rational motive: "I can't help it," Il Matto confesses. "Zampanò's such a brute." Unmindful of the danger, The Fool heckles Zampanò during his performance with the chain, in an attempt to puncture his arrogance and to disparage his strength; he also tries to use Gelsomina in his own act, much against Zampanò's wishes; and once, he even throws a bucket of water in the strongman's face. Finally, Zampanò pulls a knife on The Fool—which gesture results in his being jailed, and in both of them being fired by Colombaioni.

While Zampanò is locked up, Gelsomina has a fateful conversation with The Fool. It is night, and around the couple the circus tents are half-dismantled, for Colombaioni has decided to leave town; Gelsomina, if she chooses, can remain with the circus. She asks The Fool for advice. And it is here, because of the abstract nature of his theme, that Fellini must rely on dialogue to carry the meaning:

> *The Fool:*   So, go on, do it! It's a good chance to get rid of
> Zampanò, right? Can you imagine the look on his face
> tomorrow! . . . You want me to tell you whether or not

Zampanó (Anthony Quinn) performs for a crowd as Gelsomina watches. Quinn has said: "I learned more about film acting in three months with Fellini than I'd learned in fifty movies I'd made before then."

you should stay with him. Isn't that so? . . . I can't tell
you what to do.

Gelsomina explains how once before Zampanò had prevented
her from leaving him.

> *The Fool:* Why didn't he let you leave? No, no, all things
> considered I wouldn't take you with me, even if you
> wanted me to. Who knows . . . maybe he loves you?
> *Gelsomina:* Me, Zampanò?
> *The Fool:* Inside, he's a dog. He looks like a man . . . but
> when he tries to talk, he barks! . . . If you didn't stay
> with him, who would? I am ignorant, but I've read some
> books; so, you are not going to make me believe . . . and
> yet everything in the world is good for something.
> Take . . . take this stone, for example.
> *Gelsomina:* Which one?
> *The Fool:* Uh, this one—it doesn't matter which. Even
> this little stone has a purpose.
> *Gelsomina:* What's it good for?
> *The Fool:* Well, it's good for . . . How do I know? If I
> knew, you know who I would be?
> *Gelsomina:* Who?
> *The Fool:* God. He knows all. When you are born, when
> you die . . . I don't know what it's good for, this pebble,
> but it certainly has its use! If it were useless, then
> everything else would also be useless—even the stars!
> That's the way things are, you know. You too—you have
> your reason for being here . . .

Convinced now that her purpose in life is to remain with
Zampanò—to teach him how to love, to teach him how to be a
human being—the next morning Gelsomina bids farewell to
The Fool as she waits outside the jail near the moto-trailer for
the strongman. Separating from Il Matto is painful for
Gelsomina, inasmuch as a spiritual affinity exists between the
two (in some scenes Fellini visually suggests this close relationship by matching Gelsomina's striped jersey with The Fool's
striped trousers), but she naively believes that Zampanò will

soon change in his attitude toward her. When the brute appears
on the sidewalk beside her again, however, he has little to say
and the two resume their travels.

At about the mid-point in the structure, Fellini shows
Zampanò and Gelsomina pausing by the sea. "Where's my
home?" Gelsomina asks. Wading into the water and nodding
indifferently off to the right, Zampanò answers: "Over there."
Gelsomina smiles warmly in the sun. "I wanted to leave you
once," she tells him. "But now you're my home." Zampanò
only laughs. "Sure," he says. "With me, at least you eat
regularly." Gelsomina explodes.

This scene by the water reminds the viewer of the film's
opening, but it also prepares him for the ending.

Shot of Zampanò driving his motorcycle; behind him sit
Gelsomina and a beautiful nun. Dusk is closing in, fast. The
strongman asks the sister if he and his "wife" can stay at her
convent for the night; once there, the Mother Superior agrees
and the nun brings food to her guests. After eating, Zampanò
tells Gelsomina to play something for the sister on her trumpet.
The simple, haunting tune—so expressive of Gelsomina's
soul—delights the nun. Close-up of Zampanò's face. Anthony
Quinn's eminently plastic features reveal the complex feelings
suddenly experienced by this inarticulate boor. For the music
seems to touch something heretofore undiscovered in Zampanò:
he looks uneasy, humble, softened, bashful, embarassed. Positive forces appear to be stirring inside him. However, perhaps
Zampanò also feels threatened—not only by love, which would
alter his whole personality, but also by jealousy, for he was
always mocked Gelsomina and here she is playing in an
admirable way. When the nun begins washing the dishes, Zampanò offers to do them for her, but she won't let him. When an
elderly sister begins to split some wood, Zampanò jumps up and
takes the ax away from her. "Here, let me do that," he says.
"That's a man's work." Again, Zampanò's motivation would
seem to be complex. By offering his help, the strongman reveals
an embryonic goodness in his nature; yet, such physical
activities as washing dishes and—especially—chopping wood

also permit him to be the star of the show again. It is hard for a man like Zampanò to change.

Night. Zampanò and Gelsomina are bedding down in the convent granary. The composition—Zampanò in the foreground, lying on his side with his back to his "wife"; Gelsomina in the background, facing him across a space of ground—comprise a visual statement on the nature of the couple's relationship. Gelsomina yearns for Zampanò to take an interest in her but he only wants to sleep. "If I died," she asks, "would you be sorry?" He replies: "Why? You thinking of dying?" Exasperated, Gelsomina asks: "Don't you ever think?" He replies: "What's there to think about?" Perhaps hoping to stir him again, as well as to give vent to her feelings, Gelsomina blows on her trumpet; this time, however, Zampanò merely growls: "Knock it off!"

. . . Later that night. As lightning flashes in the granary and thunder booms outside the convent, Gelsomina wakes up. She discovers Zampanò trying to squeeze his hand through some narrow bars in an attempt to steal a few silver hearts from the wall of the adjacent chapel. He tells her to help him. Shocked by his behavior, Gelsomina refuses. The brute strikes his tiny companion, who slides down against a wall, sobbing . . . The scene fades out.

Fade in on the following morning: Zampanò and Gelsomina are preparing to leave the convent. The strongman utters a pious, hypocritical farewell: "Blessed be His name!"; however, Gelsomina is reluctant to leave this place in which women are happy because they feel useful. "Do you want to stay with us?" the young nun asks. No reply . . . for Gelsomina knows her fate. The nun attempts to console her:

> *The Nun:* We change convents every two years, so as not to forget what's most important. I mean, God. You see, we both travel. You follow your husband and I mine.
> *Gelsomina:* Yes, each one has her own.

And once more, Gelsomina drives off with Zampanò . . .

La Strada 1954

Bright sunlight. On an empty country road Zampanò and Gelsomina encounter The Fool, who is repairing a tire on his car. Still angry with the equilibrist, the strongman punches him several times, threatening him with more violence the next time they meet. Unknown to Zampanò, his blows snapped The Fool's head against the car, causing a fatal concussion. "He broke my watch . . ." are the only words The Fool can say, as he staggers off and collapses on the ground, his fingers clawing spasmodically at the earth. Gelsomina becomes hysterical. Even Zampanò is frightened. "Now I've done it!" he says. "Now I'm in for it!" Dumping the body and the car down an embankment, Zampanò quickly drives off with Gelsomina.

Significantly, the next shots—showing the couple in flight—are enacted under a wintry sky, with bare trees shaking in the wind and snow falling on distant mountain tops. Zampanò attempts to continue with his act, but Gelsomina is unable to utter: "Zam-pan-ò is here!" or to beat the drum; instead, she constantly mutters: "The Fool is hurt! The Fool is hurt!" Gelsomina is distraught because she has seen the man she loves kill another man—the very man who had given her a reason for staying with the killer. Although her words attempt to belie the reality of The Fool's death (he is merely "hurt," not dead), deep down of course she knows the truth. At night, Gelsomina refuses to allow Zampanò to sleep with her in the trailer; and in a reversal of the earlier situation, Zampanò—who is not only afraid that Gelsomina will report his crime but who is also ashamed of the guilt he sees reflected in his companion's eyes— agrees to sleep outside on the ground. Ten days go by. On a cold, sunny afternoon, while the couple are sitting against a wall of rocks and cooking soup, Gelsomina appears to return to her old self. "It's about time," Zampanò sighs, with obvious relief. But then, off in the distance, very faintly, comes the sound of a dog barking. And suddenly, Gelsomina remembers the past: "The Fool is hurt!" she begins again. Frightened by her illness, Zampanò decides to go off alone. While Gelsomina sleeps, he gathers up his few belongings, places some money beside the embers of their fire, and leaves her trumpet nearby. Pushing the moto-trailer down the road a distance, so as not to awaken Gelsomina, Zampanò vanishes from her life. . . .

Five years pass. And we next find Zampanò working in a seaside town: his hair is gray; his stomach bulges. Although he has a new woman—a more attractive woman than Gelsomina— he doesn't seem to be happy with her. After one performance, he insists on going out for a walk, alone. On the street, Zampanò hears someone humming the tune Gelsomina used to play on her trumpet; he stops, looks around expectantly—but the humming suddenly ceases. Disappointed, he moves on. Then, just as suddenly, the humming is resumed. Beyond a fence, Zampanò discovers a young woman hanging sheets on a line in the sun.

> *Zampanò:* Where did you learn that tune?
> *The Woman:* From a little creature my father found on the beach one night. She was always playing it on her trumpet. We took her in for a time . . . but she was always crying, and she never ate.
> *Zampanò:* What happened to her?
> *The Woman:* Oh, she died.

During this scene, Fellini's camera rarely shows us the woman. Either we hear her words as we watch the wash flapping in the breeze, or we watch a reaction close-up of Zampanò's face. For what is important here is not what the woman looks like, but what she is saying and the effect of what she is saying on Zampanò as he stands on the other side of the fence.

Elsewhere in the film, as noted, Gelsomina stands by a fence and learns about a dog's death. The reader will also recall that The Fool describes Zampanò as a dog who loves Gelsomina, but who can't express his love except by barking. And it was the sound of a dog barking which made Gelsomina think of The Fool again, right before Zampanò decided to desert her. It is impossible to wholly reduce the associations just catalogued to the dimensions of rational understanding. Certainly love and death remain common to the scenes and dialogue involving fences, dogs, and Gelsomina; but Gelsomina communes with the spirit of a dead beast, whereas Zampanò grieves over the loss of a creature whom he had treated like a beast. (In one scene, Gelsomina plays a duck who is shot to death by Zampanò, for the amusement of the crowd.) On one level, Fellini seems to be "saying" that, ontologically, everything that has being should be regarded as holy. On another level, he appears to be "saying" that there is a chain of being, and that animals must not be confounded with persons.

Long shot of a carnival, later that afternoon. The strongman enters the arena and proceeds to plod listlessly through his routine with the chain. Medium shot of Zampanò, as he treads in a circle, his posture slack, his gaze turned inward. Long shot of the strongman, looking small amid his surroundings . . . Fade out.

That night. Zampanò is discovered in a cafe, drunk and belligerent. With the help of some customers, the owner succeeds in tossing the strongman outside. Enraged, Zampanò heaves some barrels at his assailants and, shouting "I don't need anyone," staggers down to the beach. What follows is surely one of the most powerful and cathartic moments in the history of the cinema. Zampanò wades into the water, reminiscent of the scene in the middle of the film when he stopped with Gelsomina at the sea. Fellini has said: "In each of my films there is a character who goes through a crisis. It seems to me that the best atmosphere with which to underline this moment of crisis is a beach or a piazza at night; for silence, the emptiness of night, or the feeling that the sea is close by, brings the character into relief; this isolation allows him to be himself without any special effort."[3] At the beginning of the film the children call Gelsomina, who is standing near the water, to come home . . . But isn't Gelsomina's real home the sea? And, by wading into the sea at the end of the film, isn't Zampanò trying to find Gelsomina again?

Turning, the strongman stumbles back up the beach and collapses on the sand, breathing heavily. Once more, Anthony Quinn's face portrays a number of reactions: Zampanò gazes out at the water, then up at the sky, and then—suddenly frightened by some thought—back out to the sea. What is going through his mind? Is he thinking of The Fool and Gelsomina, and the guilt he feels for having destroyed both of them? Is he afraid that God is looking down at him? Has the thought of commiting suicide flashed through his consciousness? Pitching forward, Zampanò begins to weep, his hands clutching at the sand the way The Fool clutched at the earth when the strongman killed him. At last, Zampanò knows that he loved Gelsomina and needed her as much as she loved and needed him.

Slowly, the camera recedes and rises, leaving Zampanò looking small and alone on the beach at night. The film begins and ends by the sea; but, though the structure is in one sense circular, the opening and closing are in sharp contrast. When we first meet Zampanò, he is standing tall and strong in the sunlight, arrogantly watching Gelsomina on her knees facing the water. When we take leave of Zampanò, however, he remains prostrate before the sea, no longer proud of his strength but hardly enduring his dark night of the soul.

What Zampanò has done to Gelsomina can be described as "tragic," for no amount of tears will ever bring back the love which she once offered him and which he blindly trampled beneath his feet. Now, Zampanò finds himself alone in the universe. Nonetheless, Gelsomina's death eventually becomes the means of Zampanò's "redemption": for man is useless and alienated only if he does not know how to love everyone and everything in the universe. Such is the meaning of Gelsomina's life and death, and such is the lesson Zampanò has begun to grasp at that final moment which Aristotle called the *anagnorisis*.* What helps make *La Strada* so unforgettable is that

---

* Fellini's conception is Dostoevskian. In *The Brothers Karamazov*, Father Zossima preaches: "Love all God's creation, the whole and every grain of sand in it. Love every leaf, every ray of God's light. Love the animals, love the plants, love everything. If you love everything, you will perceive the divine mystery of things. Once you perceive it, you will begin to comprehend it better every day. And you will come at last to love the whole world with an all-embracing love . . . 'What is hell?' I maintain that it is the suffering of being unable to love."[4] In an interview with Tullio Kezich, Fellini admitted that Dostoevsky has always "fascinated" him.[5] It is worth noting that the character of "the holy fool" also appears throughout the work of Dostoevsky.

Fellini subjects not only Zampanò but also the viewer to the same recognition.

"From a sentimental point of view," Fellini has remarked, "I can say that the film I am most attached to is *La Strada*. Above all, because I feel that it is my most representative film, the one that is the most autobiographical; for both personal and sentimental reasons, because it is the film that I had the greatest trouble in realizing and that gave me the most difficulty when the time came to find a producer. Gelsomina is, naturally, my favorite among all the characters."[6] Elsewhere Fellini has added that, of all the imaginary beings he has brought to the screen, he feels closest to the three principals in *La Strada*, "especially to Zampanò."[7]

Winner of over fifty international awards (including the Grand Prize at the Venice Film Festival and the New York Film Critics and Academy Awards as the Best Foreign Film), *La Strada* remains Fellini's masterpiece and one of the greatest films every made by anyone, anywhere.

6
On the Waterfront
1954

Budd Schulberg's script for *On the Waterfront* was inspired by union corruption on the Hoboken docks. Originally, playwright Arthur Miller began a scenario on the subject entitled *The Hook* (after the longshoreman's hook), but Miller eventually lost interest in the project. In addition to taking over Miller's unpolished script, Schulberg studied Malcolm Johnson's 1949 Pulitzer Prize winning articles about the docks for the New York *Sun*. Schulberg was an experienced scenarist, in addition to having written three best-selling novels: *What Makes Sammy Run?* (1941), *The Harder They Fall* (1947), and *The Disenchanted* (1950).

Elia Kazan directed *On the Waterfront.* In the thirties, Kazan worked as an actor and director for the stage, most notably with the Group Theater. Lee J. Cobb and Karl Malden both appeared with him in the Group's 1937 production of *Golden Boy* by Clifford Odets. In 1947, Kazan co-founded with Lee Strasberg the Actor's Studio, which became famous for its "method" performances. Kazan brought the method, along with many of his pupils, to the screen.* Before filming *On the*

---

* Method acting originated with Constantin Stanislavsky and the Moscow Art Theater. Stanislavsky taught that the actor must create an "imagined truth," one which he can believe in to the same extent as he believes in "actual truth." According to Stanislavsky and his American followers, the actor must create reality through the character. He must become the character, while at the same time remaining himself to the extent that he can criticize his own performance. There is still much controversy about method acting, both from within the movement and from outside.

Waterfront, Kazan had made his reputation in the forties by directing outstanding stage plays—Tennessee Williams's *A Streetcar Named Desire* (1947), for example, and Arthur Miller's *Death of a Salesman* (1949)—as well as by directing nine films—among them the adaptation of *Streetcar* (1951) and *Viva Zapata!* (1952), both of which starred Marlon Brando.

The plot of *On the Waterfront* is simple. Terry Malloy (Marlon Brando), once a prizefighter, now almost thirty, works as a longshoreman and errand boy for Johnny Friendly (Lee J. Cobb), a corrupt union boss. At the opening of the film, Terry is sent to Joey Doyle's house to lure him up to the roof where two of Friendly's thugs kill him. Terry is distressed, because he thought the thugs were just going to "lean on" Joey, not push him off the roof. Right from the start, then, Terry is presented as a man with conscience.

Joey Doyle, who was going to "sing" to the Crime Commission, is mourned by his sister Edie (Eva Marie Saint), who vows to see the men responsible for her brother's death punished. She is assisted in her resolve by the parish priest Father Barry (Karl Malden). The longshoremen are intimidated by Friendly's thugs and they also adhere to a philosophy of "D. and D."—that is, "deaf and dumb." Anyone who reports to the Crime Commission is a "pigeon." When Terry goes to Friendly's bar to complain about Joey Doyle's death, the union leader attempts to pacify him with a soft job and a five-dollar bill. Charlie Malloy (Rod Steiger), counsel to Friendly, tells his younger brother Terry: "Hey, you got a real friend here in Johnny. Don't you forget it"; Terry says nothing.

Terry meets Edie, and the two begin to fall in love. Naturally, Edie does not know that Terry was involved in her brother's death. She realizes, however, that Terry knows enough about the docks to help put an end to Friendly's rule. Both she and the priest work on Terry's conscience. Terry is divided, on the one hand, between his love for Edie and his deep awareness of what is right, and on the other, his love for Charlie, his sense of loyalty to Friendly, and the code of "D. and D."

Terry is subpoenaed to appear before the Crime Commission. He refuses. "Kayo" Dugan, another longshoreman, agrees to tell everything he knows. Before Dugan can do so, however, Friendly has him killed, too. With prodding from the priest, Terry finally confesses to Edie that he played a part in her brother's death. At first, she runs away from him, but the couple's love for each other is so strong that they are soon reconciled. Friendly is afraid that Terry will decide to go to the Crime Commission. As a result, he sends Charlie to see Terry. His task is to buy off Terry or kill him. If Charlie does not kill Terry, then he himself will be killed. Unfortunately for Charlie, Terry refuses to commit himself, one way or the other. When Friendly has Charlie killed, Terry goes after the union boss with a gun, but Father Barry convinces Terry that the way to really hurt Johnny Friendly is for him to go before the Crime Commission. Terry agrees.

Afterward, however, everyone on the docks turns against Terry. Even though he did the right thing in appearing before the Crime Commission, he broke the code of "D. and D." Friendly sees to it that Terry is unable to get work as a longshoreman. Determined to receive his due, Terry confronts Friendly. And in front of all the workers, he tells the boss that he is glad he "ratted on him." Terry and Friendly fight. When Terry begins to get the better of it, Friendly calls in his thugs and the younger man is badly beaten. But the longshoremen are impressed by Terry's courage and integrity. Consequently, when Friendly orders them to work they refuse. Joey Doyle's father pushes the union boss into the water. If Terry can manage to stagger into work, the other longshoremen will follow him. Terry does so, and Johnny Friendly's rule on the docks is broken.

The cinematographer for *On the Waterfront* was Boris Kaufman, one of the finest technicians in the business. Like the neo-realist film-makers, Kaufman transforms an ugly reality into poetic and vivid images. Filmed on location in near zero temperatures over a nine-week period, the movie presents a heightened view of the environment, thanks to composition and lighting. Kaufman's camera seems to catch the essence of the dockside surroundings: the drab brick tenements; the garbage cans the viewer can almost smell; the rooftops cluttered with washlines, television antennas, and pigeon coops; the bare dreary little park in which winos huddle around barrels with fires in them; the dismal Roman Catholic Church, facing the park; the pale fog blowing off the Hudson, drifting across the park and the docks, bathing the action at times in a ghostly light; the dingy neighborhood saloon owned by Johnny Friendly; the barge with a little shack on it, tied up to a pier, used as an office by the union local; wet cobblestones glistening under street lamps; the cramped unprepossessing flat in which Edie and her father live—these, and other, images haunt the mind. No wonder Kazan has called Kaufman the best cameraman he has ever had.[1]

Although Kazan is an uneven director—he is addicted to melodramatic flourishes—*On the Waterfront*, taken all around, remains his best effort for the screen. Structurally, the film strikes a balance between horizontal progression of story and vertical exploration of character and theme. Throughout the picture a violent scene is followed by a quiet one. Kazan's camera moves rapidly and the editing is brisk in the action scenes, whereas in the quiet scenes—such as the love scenes—there are stationary close-ups and long takes. Thus technique, mood, and theme are mutually supporting.

At the beginning of the film, when Terry goes to Joey Doyle's house, Kazan visually foreshadows Charlie's death. Terry is standing on the street with a pigeon in his hand which he says belongs to Joey. Leaning out of his window, Joey tells Terry that he will meet him on the roof. Immediately the camera tilts up to the roof—where we see two thugs waiting for Joey. Later in the film, when Charlie is unable to convince Terry not to reveal what he knows to the Crime Commission, Kazan shows the cab in which Charlie is kidnapped by a driver in the employ of Friendly pulling into a warehouse.

Immediately, the camera tilts up to an office over the entrance to the warehouse—where we see Johnny Friendly and his thugs waiting for Charlie.

Because Charlie's murder is so important in the structure of the action—it forces Terry to react—Kazan foreshadows it visually in another way. Early in the film, Charlie comes to a warehouse to talk with his brother. Terry is seated on some coffee bags, reading a girlie magazine, his back resting against some planks, each plank about six inches apart. Charlie stands on the other side of the enclosure, looking over Terry's shoulder, his arms thrust awkwardly through the space between the planks. Later in the film, after taking two bullets in the chest, Charlie's body is spiked to a wall in an alley. When Terry lifts the body off the spike, Charlie's arms assume the same awkward position they did in the earlier scene.

Although there is much direct presentation of violence in *On the Waterfront*—we see some longshoremen being struck with baseball bats by union thugs, for example, and the showdown brawl between Terry and Friendly—Kazan exercises telling restraint. We do not see Charlie murdered. And when Joey Doyle is pushed off the roof, we are spared the sight of his body splattering on the sidewalk. Instead, we have a shot of Joey being hurled screaming from the roof, then a shot of a flapping washline which the body has passed, and finally a shot of Joey's body concealed by newspapers as people crowd around the victim. The oblique presentation of a strong action is often more effective than showing it, since it forces the viewer to use his imagination.

In scene after scene, *On the Waterfront* reveals shots of admirable symbolic value and pictorial expressiveness. When Charlie tells his brother: "Hey, you got a real friend here in Johnny," Kazan frames the retreating hero with two rows of longshoremen, their huge figures seeming to engulf the already isolated Terry. Throughout the film, pigeons are used as symbols of Terry's innate sensitivity and of the desire of the workingmen for a better life. "There are hawks in this city," Terry tells Edie. "They wait on the tops of buildings and prey

The back room of Johnny Friendly's bar in *On the Waterfront*. Friendly (Lee J. Cobb) gives some money to Terry Malloy (Marlon Brando), who is disturbed over Joey Doyle's death. Charlie Malloy (Rod Steiger) looks on. In this shot we see three of the finest actors who have worked in film.

on pigeons." Clearly, the "hawks" are people like Johnny Friendly; the "pigeons" are the rank and file longshoremen. When Joey Doyle is pushed off his roof, one thug remarks: "A canary. He could sing—but he couldn't fly." Anyone who violates the code of "D. and D." is a stool pigeon. When Terry does so, a boy who had formerly admired him breaks the necks of all his pigeons. Throwing a dead pigeon at Terry's feet, the boy cries: "A pigeon for a pigeon!" Earlier in the film, Terry shows Edie a pigeon and explains how the birds resemble human lovers in that male and female form bonds which last until death. Even though Schulberg's dialogue occasionally explains the symbolism, Kazan makes certain that the camera usually shows us the pigeons in a manner that transforms the abstractions into concrete referents.

When Terry finally tells Edie that he was involved in her brother's murder, Kazan lets us hear only a few words of the conversation. Since we already know what Terry is going to tell her there is no need for us to hear everything as the scene plays itself out. Instead, Kazan obliges us to concentrate on Edie's emotional reaction. Naturally Edie is horrified. As the truth spills from Terry's lips, Kazan keeps cutting back and forth from one face to the other, each succeeding shot tighter than the previous one. A ship's whistle—reminding us of the corrupt waterfront situation which led to Joey's murder—simulates the scream which issues from Edie's mouth and drowns out almost all of Terry's confession on the sound track. Finally, Kazan cuts to a long shot as Edie runs from Terry.

At the end of the film, when Terry is beaten up by Friendly's hoods, Kazan tilts his camera down on the fallen hero. Our seeing Terry from a high angle makes him look small—defeated and pathetic. But when the elder Doyle pushes Friendly into the water, we see the union boss falling from a high angle, too. The shot helps prepare us for Terry's triumph. After this turning point in the action, Terry proceeds to stagger past the workers, toward the warehouse. Kazan mixes objective and subjective shots. We see Terry and the crowd in long shots and medium shots: Terry's face, his feet, the faces of the men.

We see what Terry sees: the front of the warehouse, a ship owner standing in front of it—now in focus, now out of focus—as the hero struggles to retain consciousness. Finally, Terry makes it to the warehouse, pulling up the zipper on his windbreaker to shut out the cold and to keep in the blood. Since he is victorious, Kazan photographs him from a low angle, making him appear taller than usual.

The ending—the fight between Terry and Friendly, and Terry's leading the workers into the warehouse—has sometimes been called melodramatic, the technique showy. A more restrained ending may or may not have been more effective. The tension between Terry and Friendly, and between the workers and Friendly, builds up throughout the entire film. Without a confrontation scene of sufficient action and emotional power—without a dramatic revelation of the triumph of good over evil—many viewers might be left feeling that they have been denied a satisfactory catharsis. One thing is certain. No one who has seen the ending of *On the Waterfront* is likely to forget it.

Leonard Bernstein's score for the film, however, is certainly open to criticism. A melodramatic drumbeat announces the approaching death of Joey Doyle. In the tender love scenes, a symphony orchestra threatens to blow Terry and Edie off the roof, too. At times we cannot hear the dialogue, thanks to Bernstein's obtrusive, almost operatic, playing. When the cabdriver takes Charlie to his death the music comes up like thunder. Much too often, the pompous score clashes with the visuals. Even with Kazan's and Kaufman's *poetic* realism, music which would be appropriate for *Tristan and Isolde* seems out of place on the docks of Hoboken.

Perhaps the most outstanding feature of *On the Waterfront* is the acting. Kazan assembled a cast of first-rate performers, even down to some of the minor roles. Pat Hingle plays a waiter who has just a few words of dialogue; Nehemiah Persoff plays a cabdriver who doesn't speak a word; Lief Erickson and Martin Balsam play investigators for the Crime Commission. There are some nonprofessionals in the cast, too—most notably Tony Galento, Tami Mauriello, and Abe Simon, three ex-heavy-weight contenders (all of whom enjoyed the dubious distinction of having once been knocked out by Joe Louis), who under Kazan's expert direction convincingly play Friendly's thugs.

Cobb plays the corrupt union leader with a blustering viciousness. He possesses the good actor's ability to move his body in a way that makes him look bigger than he really is. In Stanislavskian terms, Friendly's "spine" is "to hold on to his leadership, whatever the cost." Friendly tells us that he was one of ten children whose mother had to scrub floors and exist on a "stinking watchman's pension." Cobb spits out the words, as though defying anyone to deny him the right to his corruption. When Friendly pulls down his collar to show Terry a scar on his neck—"See this? There was a lot of rough fellers on the way up. They gave me something to remember them by"— Cobb's mouth looks huge, as though he would devour everyone and everything that came his way. When Friendly leans over Terry's back, fondly remembering the latter's career as a boxer, his caress is but a hair's width away from a crushing blow, as Cobb makes us feel the terrible power in his hands.

Eva Marie Saint—beautiful and frail and sensitive—looks like a figure in a Fra Angelico painting. Yet for all her delicateness, her unworldliness, her convent education, Edie is portrayed as a determined and realistic young woman. Rod Steiger as Charlie projects a similarly complex character—arrogant and obsequious, educated beyond his intelligence, overdressed and spiritually undernourished, loyal to his brother but nevertheless his brother's worst enemy. And Karl Malden as Father Barry is a sensitive man who must act tough on the docks if he is to receive any respect, if he is to get his "message" across. Yet Father Barry never forgets his role as a priest. "If I squeal my life won't be worth a nickel," says Terry; to which Father Barry replies: "And if you don't squeal—what will your soul be worth?" Unfortunately, there are times when Malden's performance borders on the hammy. When Terry confesses to Edie his part in her brother's death, Kazan cuts to a shot of the priest supposedly fighting back tears—though Malden's twisted countenance suggests an actor trying to force himself to cry. In

A tender scene between Terry and Edie Doyle (Eva Marie Saint). Throughout the film pigeons are used as symbols of Terry's innate sensitivity and of the desire of the workingman for a better life.

Friendly's bar, when Father Barry talks Terry out of shooting the union leader, Malden barks to the bartender: "Gimme a beer." Here he is the movie priest, milking the audience for laughs—though, of course, the line is presumably Schulberg's.

The most impressive performance in the film, however, is Brando's Terry Malloy. It has often been said that movie actors do not really act. Didn't the filmed experiments of the influential Russian aesthetician Lev Kuleshov earlier in the century prove that montage was everything? In one case, Kuleshov created a woman who had no counterpart in reality. He shot the face, hair, hands, legs, and feet of different women, but because of the editing, he conveyed the illusion of one woman grooming herself before a mirror. In another case, Kuleshov followed a single, expressionless close-up of an actor with three shots: 1) a plate of soup, 2) a coffin containing a woman's body, and 3) a little girl playing with a toy. Viewers shown the results praised the actor's performance, although his expression never changed. He did not look hungry; he did not look sad; he did not look happy. Kuleshov and others concluded that it is irrelevant how the actor works. Didn't Eisenstein and De Sica succeed with many nonprofessionals in their casts?

There seem to be two kinds of films—those that do not require acting in the usual sense and those that do. Some would even argue that, as good as Eisenstein's and De Sica's films are, they would even be better with sturdy professionals in them. Frank Sinatra, who had wanted the part of Terry Malloy, was outraged when Brando got the role instead. As Stanley Kauffmann has observed: "the emotion displayed by Sinatra . . . is always Sinatra's emotion, not the character's . . . He simply behaves in any part as he would behave in life . . . If it were possible to see Sinatra in Brando's role in *On the Waterfront*, it would clarify the difference between mere simulation and creative acting."[2] Brando proves that movie actors sometimes *do* act.

As Terry Malloy, Brando has the thick muscular body of an athlete; still, he is extremely graceful. He has the head of a

Roman gladiator, yet his face—even with the scar tissue over the eyes and the ridge across the nose—remains sensitively expressive. Brando, who visited the old Stillman's Gym on Eighth Avenue in New York City to study boxers, is thoroughly convincing as a former pugilist. He has the fighter's walk—the feet close together, the weight balanced on the balls of the feet, the movements cat-like. His shoulders and arms suggest a restrained power, the strength that comes from years of work on the pulleys and from hitting the light and heavy bags.

Terry Malloy is not a bright man. Brought up in an orphanage, schooled in the jungle code of the streets—"Wanna know my philosophy?" he tells Edie. "Get the other guy before he gets you"—Terry nevertheless has a decent nature which slowly responds to Edie's love and Father Barry's preaching. Brando projects Terry's inner conflict through the way he shrugs his shoulders, hands jammed into his pockets, too inarticulate to enunciate his torment. Unable to tell Edie that he is attracted to her, he playfully slips on her glove as they walk in the park; unable to tell her at first that she is beautiful, he makes fun of the way she looked as a child. He covers his deep feelings of inferiority by acting cocky, chewing gum in an arrogant manner. Thinking for this ex-fighter is a real effort. Brow drawn painfully, eyes blinking, Terry struggles valiantly in his search for the right course of action.

In the role of Terry Malloy, Brando often mumbles so as not to appear overly articulate. Eloquence would be out of character. Frequently, he expresses a feeling or an emotion with a gesture instead of words. And speaking of words, Brando uses cue cards because he thinks memorizing lines has a deadening effect on acting. In real life, a person often doesn't know what he is going to say until he says it. The actor, Brando, believes, should aim for spontaneity. If the actor waits for his turn to speak, and then looks at a cue card, what he says will appear more natural, less rehearsed.

Perhaps the most famous scene in *On the Waterfront*—the one which well might be the greatest triumph of Brando's career—is also the least "cinematic," at least insofar as that word is generally understood. When Charlie attempts to persuade Terry not to appear before the Crime Commission, the scene is shot in the back of a taxi.* It is a long scene, and there is no camera movement or quick cutting or physical action by the two characters. Only three different shots are used: a medium shot of Terry and Charlie, a close-up of Terry, and a close-up of Charlie. Kazan has a shade drawn on the rear window of the cab so that we are not distracted by the sight of other vehicles. For the same reason, we are never given profile shots of the two brothers, for in that case we might see out the windows of the cab. We do not even see the cabdriver until the scene is nearly over. What is happening in the back seat remains extremely important, and Kazan wishes to focus our attention on it completely.

Terry has a recognition scene: Charlie did not love him enough—he was not a real brother. The revelation begins when Charlie, after failing to get Terry to agree not to confess what he knows before the Crime Commission, says: "You could've been another Billy Conn, slugger. It was that rotten manager you had."

"My manager?" Terry replies incredulously. "Remember that night in the Garden? You came down to my dressing room and said, 'Kid, this ain't your night. We're goin' for the price on Wilson.' Remember that? 'This ain't your night.' *My night!*" Recalling it now, all the pain comes rushing back, and as Brando plays him there is almost a sob in Terry's throat. "I coulda taken Wilson apart! So what happens? He gets the title shot outdoors in the ballpark and what do I get? A one-way ticket to Palookaville. You was my brother, Charlie, you should of looked after me a little bit."

Guiltily, Charlie protests. "I had some bets down for you . . . You saw some money."

"You don't understand," says Terry. "I coulda had class. I

---

* It has been said that this scene was improvised by Brando and Steiger.

coulda been a contender. I coulda been somebody—instead of a bum—which is what I am. Let's face it. It was you, Charlie."

Terry is not angry, just sad. And Brando's slight underplaying of the scene—never raising his voice, never revealing bitterness, almost tender toward his faithless brother, his strong feelings held in check—is much more effective than if he had torn his "passion to tatters."

When Charlie pulls a gun on Terry, the latter shakes his head as though he can't believe what his eyes see. Gently, he turns the weapon aside and, shaking his head, sadly emits a "Wow" with all the beauty and profound feeling of a line from Shakespeare.

"Okay," Charlie says, wearily. "Okay, I'll tell Johnny Friendly I couldn't find you. Ten to one he won't believe me." And in Steiger's eyes we see fear, a glimpse of the fate he knows awaits him. However, he at least shows more concern for his brother than for himself. He hands Terry the gun. "Here—take this. You're going to need it." Then, to the cabdriver, he says: "You, you pull over."*

Brando uses himself as Terry Malloy in a way that few actors have ever done on the screen. He is thoroughly convincing as the character, yet we are always aware that a great actor is playing a part. Brando knows what he is doing, and that gives the viewer an aesthetic pleasure. It is method acting at its finest.

Kazan and Schulberg state the theme of *On the Waterfront* in an opening title: "It has always been in the American tradition not to hide our shortcomings, but on the contrary, to spotlight them and to correct them. The incidents portrayed in this picture were true of a particular area of the waterfront. They exemplify the way self-appointed tyrants can be fought and defeated by right-thinking men in a vital democracy." The filmmakers put flesh on this theme through the inner struggle of

---

* This excellent scene ends clumsily when Kazan shows "Terry" getting out of the cab in a long shot. The actor is clearly not Brando. Furthermore, "Terry"—who had been sitting on the driver's side—gets out on the right side of the cab.

Terry to gain a sense of his own identity—"All those years," he tells Friendly, "I was ratting on myself"—and of his obligation to society—"There's more to this than I thought, Charlie," he says to his brother in the back of the cab.

In *On the Waterfront*, two approaches to the problem of corruption are presented. The film "says" that all men are brothers in Christ, that the murder of a workingman is a form of crucifixtion, and that at the end Terry is a kind of redemptive Christ figure. Father Barry articulates much of the Christian philosophy in the film. His character was based on a real priest who became involved in reform of the Hoboken waterfront.

On the Waterfront also "says" that evil can be destroyed by collective action, but only if a leader shows the way. Although Father Barry is the ideologue, it is Terry Malloy who translates theory into action. Since the character played by Brando is not seen as particularly religious, his action for the most part can be viewed in secular terms, although at times— such as at the conclusion—he does appear to move within a Christian ambience.

There is a conflict between these two thematic elements only in the minds of those Christians who claim a monopoly on virtue, those secularists who abhor religion, and Marxists who not only abhor religion but also abhor any suggestion of individualistic as opposed to collectivist action.

True, in reality corruption on the docks of Hoboken was allowed to persist for so long because there was also corruption elsewhere in society. Kazan and Schulberg never intended, however, for *On the Waterfront* to be a study in depth of all the forces responsible for the existence of a Johnny Friendly. During the Crime Commission hearings, Kazan cuts to a shot of a fat man watching the proceedings on television. Distressed by what he sees, the man tells his servant to turn off the set and not to accept any more calls from Mr. Friendly. From this intercut, the audience knows that the longshoremen's union could prevail in its wrongdoings only because of greedy shipowners, venal politicians, and crooked policemen. The structure of the film—

its unified dramatic impact—would have been destroyed by a more ambitious social perspective.

After over twenty years, *On the Waterfront* remains one of the most powerful American films ever made.*

---

* Today Hoboken is no longer the port it was when *On the Waterfront* was made. Most of the corruption no longer exists. The character of Terry Malloy was based on Anthony (Tony Mike) De Vincenzo, who collected over $25,000 in an out-of-court settlement after charging the movie-makers with invasion of privacy. Several years ago, Mr. De Vincenzo remarked: "I was proud to be a rat. The men I fought are dead and buried and God bless them, but Tony Mike is alive" (quoted in *The New York Times*, May 24, 1973).

7
Wild Strawberries
1957

Ingmar Bergman's *Wild Strawberries*, one of the Swedish director's finest films, had its genesis in a personal experience. In the autumn of 1956, when he was thirty-eight, Bergman drove to the university town of Uppsala, where he had lived as a boy with his grandmother. On an impulse, he revisited his grandmother's old house. Bergman stood there, his hand on the doorknob, thinking: If I open it—could I walk back into my childhood? It was then that Bergman got the idea for a film. Suppose he made a realistic picture about someone who could go back in time, who could relive certain experiences and conjure up people who were long dead. Thus was born *Wild Strawberries*.[1]

Bergman, who began writing the script in the spring of 1957, decided that the name of his central character would be Isak Borg. He selected the name Isak because the character was "icy." Only later did Bergman realize that Isak Borg had the same initials as the director himself.[2] But gradually it occurred to Bergman that an old man should be the main character, and that the best actor for the part would be Victor Sjöström, who Andrew Sarris once suggested may possibly have been "the world's first great director, even before Chaplin and Griffith."[3] Sjöström, who made several films in the United States, was nearly eighty when *Wild Strawberries* appeared; he died in 1960. His contribution to the success of the film was an enormous one, perhaps because he too was able to identify with Isak Borg.*

The action in *Wild Strawberries* covers a time span in the present of about twenty-four hours. Thanks to his expressionistic techniques, or the stream-of-consciousness subject matter, however, Bergman encompasses almost the entire lifetime of the seventy-eight-year-old Borg, a professor of medicine.

Structure in the film, then, is complex. On one level, *Wild Strawberries* proceeds horizontally. Professor Borg drives by car from Stockholm to Lund, where he will receive an honorary degree at the university. Like Fellini, Bergman uses the road as a symbol for man's journey through life. During the journey, Borg meets various people and revisits different places which he knew in the past, and these occurrences permit Bergman to explore the old man's inner life. Hence, the forward progress of the story in present time is halted at key points in the film—that is, the structure becomes vertical—so that we can enter Borg's mind. Since the past is as much Bergman's subject as the present, however, there is no question of the vertical dimension slowing the pace of the film. There is perfect unity of action.

In his construction of *Wild Strawberries*, Bergman was influenced by the Swedish playwright August Strindberg, especially by his *A Dream Play* (1912).† As an early expressionist, Strindberg had attempted to break out of the confines of a narrow realism, to project inner reality on the stage. The form of *A Dream Play* is not logical—time and space vanish. Structure develops according to the laws of the unconscious. In his preface to the play, Strindberg says: "On a flimsy foundation of actual happenings, imagination spins, and weaves in new patterns: an intermingling of remembrances, experiences, whims, fancies, ideas, fantastic absurdities and improvisations, and

---

* Bergman has described Sjöström as "misanthropic."[4] It has also been said that in 1916, during a difficult time in his life, Sjöström made a bicycle journey to that part of his country where he had lived as a child.[5]

† In 1977, Bergman directed *A Dream Play* at the Residenz Theater in Munich.

original inventions of the mind."[6] To a large extent, Strindberg's preface could be attached to *Wild Strawberries*.

The development of film art owes a great deal to the stream-of-consciousness novelists—James Joyce, Virginia Woolf, and William Faulkner. Although the novel is better able to reveal the stream of consciousness and the camera is better equipped to record the stream of physical events, both forms of art can deal with inner and outer reality. That the novel and the film have much in common is borne out by the enormous borrowing between the two mediums in the last sixty odd years. Flashbacks generally retard the tempo of a novel or film, because they interrupt the forward motion of the story in order to explain something laboriously. Today, flashbacks in the novel and film have become less and less employed in solid blocks of exposition, but are instead projected in fragments, in sudden bursts of recollection, smoothly woven into the fabric of the present moment. In some recent films, the remembrance of things past lasts no longer than a split second on the screen, being cut in and out of the present with dazzling swiftness.

Naturally, a philosophical revolution, with its roots in our altered perception of time and our awareness of the relationship between the conscious and unconscious levels of our mind, is one of the factors operating on modern narrative development. The past used to be tidily packaged within a long coherent flashback. Once the thought of William James, Sigmund Freud, and Henri Bergson became known, however, writers and film-makers responded by fusing past and present, by showing how memories exist dynamically and meaningfully in the mind of a fictional character here and now. Bergman's *Wild Strawberries* is within this narrative tradition, even though the stream-of-consciousness portions of the action tend to be somewhat longer than is often the case today.

A description of the action in *Wild Strawberries* is necessary before we can analyze its parts. On the day he is to be honored by receiving a degree, Professor Borg wakes up, disturbed by a nightmare involving his own death. This nightmare provides the charge which prompts Borg to examine his values, his past and present life, and his relationships with people. Miss Agda (Jullan Kindahl), his old housekeeper, and Marianne (Ingrid Thulin), his daughter-in-law, both accuse him of being selfish and egotistical. Borg decides to drive to Lund with Marianne—who has temporarily separated from her husband; his car resembles a hearse.

On the way, Borg stops at the house where he lived as a child. Here, while Marianne takes a swim, the old man visits a strawberry patch and recalls his rejection by the sweetheart of his youth, Sara (Bibi Andersson). When the journey resumes, Borg and Marianne pick up three passengers—one girl and two boys—who are on their way to Italy. The girl's name is Sara (also played by Bibi Andersson), one of the boys is named Anders (Folke Lundquist), the other Viktor (Björn Bjelvenstram). Both boys are in love with Sara. This triangle recreates the pattern from Borg's past, since he lost *his* Sara to his brother Sigfrid (Per Sjöstrand).

Shortly after picking up the three youngsters, Borg is involved in an accident. Fortunately, no one is hurt. But the couple in the other car are obliged to squeeze in with Borg and his passengers. The man's name is Alman (Gunner Sjöberg), his wife's name is Berit (Gunnel Brostrom). Because the couple hate each other and quarrel in the car, Marianne orders them out.

Borg stops at a gas station, and here he meets two people—Akerman (Max von Sydow) and his wife Eva (Anne-Mari Wiman)—the couple who own the station and who remember him from the past with affection. Afterward Borg and Marianne and the three youths have lunch at an inn. Then the old professor takes Marianne to visit his mother (Naima Wifstrand), a cold and complaining woman.

Later Borg dozes in the car and dreams again of the strawberry patch. He sees Sara and Sigfrid happily married. Then Alman returns to administer a test which Borg fails. Leading him into a forest, Alman shows Borg a couple having intercourse. The woman is Karin (Gertrude Fridh), Isak's late wife.

Again, we are told—this time from the mouth of Karin—that the professor is a cold man.

Finally, the group reach the university where Borg is to receive his honorary degree. As the day ends, old Borg tries to establish new relationships with Agda, Marianne, his son Evald (Gunnar Björnstrand), who is also a doctor, and presumably others as well. The film ends with another dream—this one pleasant. Borg returns to his childhood home and the old strawberry patch. In his dream, Borg lightheartedly observes a scene from the past in which his mother and father and the rest of the family are all having a good time.

Wild Strawberries is a film narrated by Borg. Before the credits appear, we see the old professor writing at his desk, we hear the sound of his voice on the sound track. He is writing the story of the film. Now and then, in the course of the action, Borg speaks to us from off screen. At the end, we hear him again as the first-person narrator. *Wild Strawberries* is no *Lady in the Lake* (1946),* however, in which a subjective camera replaces the hero throughout the film. Although Bergman does use a subjective camera at certain times in the picture, we generally see Borg as we see the other characters. For the most part, Bergman visually differentiates between inner and outer reality, or between those scenes which take place in Borg's mind and those which take place in the world "out there." But he does not differentiate between objective and subjective shots in external reality. When Borg gazes at Marianne, for example, the shot is as objective as when Marianne gazes at Borg. Bergman does not alter the pictorial quality of the image as he shifts from one subjective point of view to another in those scenes set in the outer world. Nevertheless, old Borg's role as the narrator tends to shape our response to the action, since everything *seems* to be seen from his angle of vision. The first-person point of view not only acts as a unifying factor in the structure of events—this is especially important in an episodic

---

* Directed by Robert Montgomery.

Sara (Bibi Andersson), the sweetheart of Borg's youth, sits in the strawberry patch with Sigfrid (Per Sjöstrand), Borg's brother. This shot is an example of Borg's remembrance of things past.

film which moves between inner and outer reality—but also reinforces the thematic content of the film. *Wild Strawberries* is about a man who, in his own words, has "withdrawn almost completely from society." Hence, the first-person mode is ideally suited to convey Borg's state of mind, because it produces an effect of individuality and separateness.

After the prologue, in which Borg introduces himself to the viewer, the film proper begins. What we see is a dream. Since, as noted, the film ends with another dream, the structure is circular. There is, however, an important difference between the two dreams—the first one is a nightmare, the second a joyous experience. In the nightmare which opens the film, Bergman's cameraman, Gunnar Fischer, creates a visual effect reminiscent of the old German expressionist film *The Cabinet of Dr. Caligari* (1921), directed by Robert Wiene. Fischer uses a high contrast film stock which creates hard black and white images which look overexposed. In this way, Bergman distinguishes the subjective world—or the dream state—from the objective world.

In Borg's nightmare, we see him taking his usual morning stroll on the street; however, the dream differs from reality in that there are no people on the street. Bergman seems to be suggesting that Borg's life is empty, that he lives in a world which excludes others. Although the sun is shining, Borg feels cold. Later in the film, when Borg visits his mother, she says: "I've always felt chilly as long as I can remember . . . Mostly in the stomach."* Here, Bergman is posing perhaps the central thematic questions of *Wild Strawberries*: How can the emotional coldness passed on within a family from generation to generation—for Borg's son, Evald, is a cold man, too—finally be stopped? Is man determined by heredity and environment—or is he free to reverse the source of his life and to creatively reshape himself into a warm and loving person?

In his nightmare, Borg stops underneath the sign of a watchmaker-optometrist. Suspended overhead is a clock without

---

* Bergman has said: "The notion occurred to me that some children are born from cold wombs. I think it's a horrible idea, little embryos lying there shivering with cold. It was out of that line of dialogue that the mother came into being."[7]

hands and a pair of eyeglasses which have broken lenses. The clock without hands suggests that time has run out for old Borg; for when he looks at his own watch, he sees that it is also without hands. Later in the film, the professor's mother shows him his late grandfather's gold watch—and it too has lost its hands. Death comes to every man. And the smashed eyeglasses symbolize the fact that Borg as yet has failed to see the truth about life and death. On the sound track there is silence except for the beating of Borg's heart. The protagonist is only a heartbeat away from the silence of the grave.

Just then, Borg notices a man standing with his back to him. But when the man turns around, Borg sees that his face is stitched together like a dummy's. And when the "man" collapses to the sidewalk, he leaves behind only a little dark fluid and a pile of clothes. Again, Borg is confronted with an image of himself.

A hearse passes. One wheel comes loose and rolls toward Borg. Frightened he steps aside. The hearse dips and a coffin slides onto the street and opens. Borg approaches; he gazes inside. Here Bergman uses a subjective camera to intensify our experience. For what Borg sees inside the coffin is himself. Suddenly the corpse reaches up for Borg and begins to pull him into the coffin. But Borg is not yet ready for death.

And at that point, he wakes up—Bergman uses a cut— shaken by his nightmare.

When Borg, later in the film, shows Marianne his childhood home, Bergman again takes us inside the old man's mind. This time Borg has a daydream—part recollection, part fantasy. Seated in the old strawberry patch, Borg recalls the past. Here Bergman uses a dissolve from the objective to the subjective. Unlike the nightmare, however, this scene glows with light. It too is stylized, but in a less obvious manner. We are informed that little Isak is out fishing with his father. Yet the old Isak observes what is going on, in and around the house.

Borg sees his childhood sweetheart—cousin Sara—picking strawberries. Then his brother Sigfrid comes along; and, after some flirting on both sides, he kisses Sara. The girl observes that she has spilled the berries and stained her white dress. Only gradually, in the course of the film, does Bergman make clear what the wild strawberries symbolize.

The action within the daydream swings to the breakfast table. Present are Borg's nine brothers and sisters, Sara, his aunt and Uncle Aron. Missing from this idyllic scene are Borg and his parents. Like Sara, everyone is dressed in dazzling white; the tablecloth is white; the room is inundated with sunlight. It is Uncle Aron's name day (the day of the saint after whom a person is named); as a result, almost everyone seems to be in a fine mood. Since Uncle Aron is deaf, he holds an earhorn to his head, and there is much good-natured joking at his expense. For example, two twins sing a song for Uncle Aron which he cannot hear. It is a romantic vision of a simple past, of a golden age which will never come again. It is set up against modern society—where there is little innocence or love—and against the darkness of the hall in which Borg stands observing the breakfast scene. The shadows of death are gathering for Borg.

When the twins tell everyone that they saw Sigfrid kissing Sara, she leaves the table in tears. Outside in the hall, she tells her sister Charlotta: "Isak . . . is so enormously refined and moral and sensitive and he wants us to read poetry together and he talks about the after-life and wants to play duets on the piano and he likes to kiss only in the dark and he talks about sinfulness. I think he is extremely intellectual and morally aloof . . . And then I think he's a child even if we are the same age, and then Sigfrid is so fresh and exciting." Subsequently, Sara married Sigfrid and had six children.

Borg comes out of his daydream—Bergman uses a cut again—and finds the second Sara standing in front of him. By having the same actress play both Saras, and by having two girls with the same name, Bergman risks departing from credibility. The aesthetic gain, however, is worth the gamble. In a stream-of-consciousness film, the artistic problem is to provide continuity between present and past actions. Bibi Andersson helps provide the necessary formal coherence. Thematically, the second Sara reinforces Borg's own insight in his daydream; that is, she causes the old man to evaluate his cold personality—the personality which led to his loss of the first Sara.

Even the two young men traveling with the second Sara, as noted, reconstitute the original triangle of the first Sara, Isak, and Sigfrid. Anders plans to become a parson (he is like the young Isak, then, in that he is concerned with morality, the after-life, and sinfulness); Viktor will become a doctor (he is like Sigfrid in that Isak's brother seemed to have contempt for conventional morality). Although Isak became a doctor and not a parson, and although the old Borg is noncommittal on whether he believes in God, he is still very much the same as when he was a young man. Unconsciously, however, Borg has tried to identify in some ways with his more sensual brother. For example, when the first Sara complains that Sigfrid smokes "smelly cigars," he defends himself by saying: "That's a man's smell, isn't it?" Old Borg tells Marianne that cigars are "a manly vice." But Borg's mother—who has always been "cold"—hates the smell of tobacco. If Borg had been more like his brother, perhaps he would have had a more satisfying life.

Similarly, the quarreling Almans are brought into the present action to remind Borg of his marriage. Later in the film, he tells Marianne that he could see his past mirrored in the Alman's mutual hatred. Marianne, who is pregnant with a child that Evald does not want, remains fearful that her own marriage will become like that of the Almans. Isak says that Evald was a product of a bad marriage. But Marianne—who bears within herself not only a new life but Bergman's symbol of love and warmth and hope for the future—points out an important difference between Isak's marriage and her own. She says: "But we love each other."

The symbolism of the wild strawberries becomes plainer if we read the screen-play. When Isak stops at the gas station, he learns that Eva is, like Marianne, pregnant. Bergman writes of Eva: "She squinted in the sun and beamed like a big strawberry in her red dress."[8] Obviously, wild strawberries are a positive symbol for life in the film. The fruit is associated with the first

Sara (who is picking berries when we see her for the first time), the second Sara (who meets Isak in the strawberry patch), the pregnant Eva, and the pregnant Marianne. These warm women are in contrast to Isak's cold mother. Nicodemus asked Jesus: "How can a man be born when he is old? Can he enter a second time into his mother's womb and be born again?"; to which Jesus replied: "That which is born of the flesh is flesh; and that which is born of the spirit is spirit." Even if Borg could enter his mother's womb a second time, he would again shiver with cold. Rebirth is possible only on the spiritual and emotional planes.

Borg and his companions next have lunch in an outdoor restaurant on Lake Vättern. As the scene opens, the group have just finished eating, and they are drinking wine and talking. The theme of the scene is man's search for love. Anders recites: "Oh, when such beauty shows itself in each facet of creation, then how beautiful must be the eternal source of this emanation!" Viktor objects to the religious poem; he argues that modern man believes in himself in spite of his insignificance. But Anders believes that modern man needs God because he cannot bear to face his emptiness without Him. When Borg is asked whether he is a believer or not, he refuses to answer. Instead he quotes as follows:

> *Borg:* "Where is the friend I seek everywhere? Dawn is the time of loneliness and care. When twilight comes, when twilight comes . . ." What follows after that Anders?
>
> *Marianne:* "When twilight comes I am still yearning."
>
> *Anders:* "Though my heart is burning, burning. I see His trace of glory . . ."
>
> *Sara:* Are you religious, Professor?
>
> *Borg:* "I see His trace of glory and power, In an ear of grain and the fragrance of flower . . ."
>
> *Marianne:* "In every sign and breath of air. His love is there. His voice whispers in the summer breeze . . ."

Everyone is moved by the expression of longing in the poem. Even Viktor concedes that—as a mere love poem—it is

In present time, Borg (Victor Sjöström) is presented with a bouquet of wild-flowers by the three young people who have traveled with him to Lund.

not too bad. As a clergyman's son, Bergman has devoted many of his films to the subject of God. Unfortunately, his search for God has proved futile. The debate over whether God exists or not can never be satisfactorily resolved on the intellectual level. (Anders and Viktor try to settle the matter by engaging in a fist fight.) In the lunch by the sea, Bergman appears to be "saying" that whether God answers man's call for Him or not, man must still learn to love life and himself and others. Man is not insignificant so long as he remains able to love.

As Borg and Marianne are about to enter his mother's house, the sky suddenly—and symbolically—turns overcast. Inside, Borg's mother complains about her ten children, twenty grandchildren, and fifteen great-grandchildren. According to her—and she may be right—none of her relatives love her. But she seems not to love them, either. She does not see her family as persons; for example, she recalls her children by the toys they played with when they were small. She refers to the toys, which she has kept, as "rubbish." No one ever comes to see her. In the modern world, the family structure has broken down, thus isolating the individual. This isolation increases one's need for love. Obviously, Borg's mother proves that the mere fact one gives birth to a child is no magic solution to the problem of loneliness. Bergman avoids the trap of mawkishness. Where there is life, there must be love.

Throughout the scene in which Borg visits his mother, Bergman again and again turns his camera on Marianne. She stares at the old lady with a look of incomprehension and disgust. It seems clear that her experience with Borg's mother will strengthen her in the resolve to have her own baby, in spite of Evald's objections, and to give her own child warmth and love. Marianne will attempt to put an end to the coldness which has been passed down from generation to generation in the Borg family.

The next subjective scene begins when, with Marianne drinking, Isak dozes off beside her. Once more, he is back at the wild strawberry patch. This time, however, the mood is different. Shots of birds flying across a murky sky, their shrill cries sounding ominous. Dissolve to a basket of strawberries spilled on the ground. In the earlier scene, Sara had overturned the strawberries and stained her white dress when Sigfrid kissed her. Some critics have read a symbolism of lost innocence in the soiled dress. But such an interpretation does not square with the way Sara is viewed by Borg throughout the film. True, after Sigfrid kisses Sara, she says melodramatically: "You've turned me into a bad woman, at least *nearly.*" The remark is intended to be funny, and not even the puritanical Borg would take it seriously. Perhaps the stained dress is just a stained dress. (As Freud said once: "Sometimes a cigar is just a cigar.") The strawberries spilled on the ground, however, do seem to suggest Borg's missed opportunities in life.

Sara appears and speaks to old Borg—a basket of strawberries on the ground between them. This would seem to be a symbol of hope. Sara shows Borg his reflection in a mirror. He looks old and ugly to himself. "In spite of all your knowledge," she says, "you don't really know anything." Sara runs off, through a howling wind, to a cradle. In it lies her sister Sigbrith's baby. Sara comforts the infant: "I'm with you. I'm holding you tight." Here perhaps Borg is torturing himself with a vision of all that he has lost. Sara could have comforted him, could have been the mother of his child. As we have seen, the wild strawberry patch and Sara are associated with the idea of love. Yet in this scene there are images of death, too—the dark birds, the gloomy sky, the shadows on the ground, the bare trees, the portentous music—for old Borg is near the end of time.

Then, suddenly, the door of a house opens and Sigfrid calls to Sara. She rushes off with the child, and disappears into the house. The birds vanish, the wind subsides. As Borg moves towards the house—the camera moving with him—we hear Sara playing the piano, we see the windows of the house lighted warmly. Borg gazes inside. He sees Sara and Sigfrid enjoying a romantic dinner together. This too—Borg is telling himself in his dream—might have been his had he been a warmer, more loving person. The lights die in the room. And Borg is left standing outside in the darkness.

Angrily, Borg knocks on the door with his left hand and holds on to the post of the doorframe with his right. Painfully, he withdraws his right hand. A nail has pierced his palm. This wound is a symbol of Borg's emotional suffering, of his private crucifixion.

The door of the house opens and Alman beckons Borg inside. They enter a lecture hall. Anders, Viktor, the second Sara, and seven other people are in attendance. Now Borg, the old professor, is himself examined by the obnoxious Alman. In the first test, Borg looks through a microscope but sees only his own eye. This suggests that Borg is entirely self-centered, that he sees only himself. In the second test, Borg is asked to explain some nonsense written on the blackboard. When the old man confesses that he cannot understand it, he is told: "On the blackboard is written the first duty of a doctor . . . A doctor's first duty is to ask forgiveness." Here Borg's guilt feelings over his lack of love find expression. In the final test, Borg examines a woman—it is Berit Alman—and claims that she is dead. However, she suddenly begins to laugh derisively. Alman's judgment is that Borg remains incompetent. In his dream, the professor is mocking the ceremony in which he will become a Jubilee Doctor. Although the academic world honors him, Borg knows that those close to him realize his "incompetence" as a human being.

Next Alman takes Borg into a dark woods. In a clearing of the woods, Borg watches his wife Karin (she has been dead for thirty years) copulating in a crude fashion with an unidentified man. Afterward Karin says that when she goes home and confesses to her husband, he will say: "You shouldn't ask forgiveness from me, I have nothing to forgive." But Borg is not being charitable. What motivates his "forgiveness" is indifference. It is he who should ask forgiveness of his dead wife.

As the dream ends, Alman passes sentence on Borg (it is,

of course, old Borg passing judgment on himself). The penalty for a life lived without love is loneliness.

When Borg returns to the objective world, he finds himself alone in the car with Marianne. Although it is raining, the three young people—ironically—are picking flowers in honor of Borg's award. "It's really strange," the protagonist remarks of his dreams. "It's as if I'm trying to say something to myself which I won't listen to when I'm awake." And when Marianne asks: "And what's that?" Borg replies: "That I'm dead—although I'm alive." Marianne says that Evald feels the same way.

Like father, like son.

Bergman then introduces a flashback. Moving his camera in close to Marianne, he has her remember another rainy day in her car when she was with Evald. When Bergman pulls his camera back, Marianne is wearing different clothes but she still occupies the driver's side of the car, whereas Evald now sits where his father had sat prior to the flashback. Although there is a shift here in viewpoint, Bergman has Borg say: "I have attempted to recall Marianne's story as accurately as possible." Since the whole film is "seen" from Borg's point of view, Marianne's story is intended to be the hero's imaginative visualization of what she told him. By having father and son sit in the same positions, by having both scenes occur in an automobile, by having rain in both scenes, Bergman is not merely pointing up the relationship between the generations; he is also making the shift in viewpoint—the flashback transition within the first-person narrative—as smooth as possible.

In the scene between Marianne and Evald, we learn that Isak's son does not want his wife to bring new life into the world. "I was an unwanted child in a marriage that was like hell. Can the old man be certain I'm really his son?" he says. "I'm disgusted by life. I don't want a responsibility which will oblige me to exist one day longer than I want to." Marianne insists that her husband is morally and philosophically in error. But Evald replies: "Nothing can be called right or wrong. You function according to your needs—you can find that out in an elementary-school textbook."* Evald adds that, whereas Marianne has a need to create life, he has a need to be dead.

Bergman ends the flashback on a close shot of Marianne—the way he began it—and then pulls his camera back, as before, this time to reveal old Borg instead of Evald. Marianne tells her father-in-law that she remains determined to have the baby, even though she loves Evald more than anyone in the world. Somehow, she argues, the emotional coldness in the Borg family, the death-in-life, must come to an end.

The scene concludes with Sara, Anders, and Viktor coming up to the car window and offering flowers to old Borg. Slowly, Bergman blacks out the area surrrounding Borg—Marianne, the three young people, the interior of the car, all vanish. And Borg is isolated, left alone to consider how he should live in the brief time remaining to him.

Next we see Borg and his companions arriving at Evald's house in Lund. Agda, Borg's housekeeper, is there, having made the journey by plane. Although they are both nervous, Marianne and Evald seem happy to see each other again. Bergman then shows Borg receiving his honorary degree at the cathedral. The pomp of the ceremony contrasts with the inner emptiness which Borg feels.

When he returns to Evald's house, Borg makes a determined effort to become a different person. His behavior is low-key and wholly credible. In Bergman's world—as in the real world as opposed to the world of bad films—human beings do not undergo instantaneous transformations. Throughout *Wild Strawberries*, the viewer has been subtly prepared for Borg's change of heart. For example, early in the picture, when Borg and Marianne commence their journey together, the old man tells his daughter-in-law not to smoke. "I can't stand cigarette smoke," he says. But later on, as Borg begins to warm in his feelings towards Marianne—to be precise, after the flash-

---

* Bergman has written: "Philosophically, there is a book which was a tremendous experience for me: Eiono Kaila's *Psychology of the Personality*. His thesis that man lives strictly according to his needs—negative and positive—was shattering to me, but terribly true. And I build on this ground."[9]

back scene—he tells her: "If you want to smoke a cigarette, you may." Similarly, Marianne begins to change in her feelings toward Borg. When they begin their trip to Lund, Marianne is not interested in hearing about her father-in-law's dreams, but later in the action, she evinces concern about his anxieties.

Borg's initial attempts to establish new relationships with people does not meet with quick success. He tries to persuade Agda that they have known each other long enough to use the intimate "*du*" when speaking to each other. But Agda wants no "intimacies," she says. "A woman must guard her reputation." The young people—Sara, Anders, and Viktor—have responded to Borg. However, they must continue their journey to Italy. And in a touching farewell, Sara tells Borg: "Do you know—it's really you I love. Today, tomorrow, and always."

When Evald comes into his father's room to say goodnight, he reports that Marianne plans to stay with him again.

Evald: I can't be without her.
Borg: You mean, you can't live alone.
Evald: I can't be without *her* . . . It will be as she wants.
Borg: And if she wants . . . Does she want?
Evald: She says she'll think it over. I don't really know.

At the beginning of the film, it was established that Borg had loaned Evald a substantial amount of money in order to complete his medical studies. Evald has been paying his father back ever since he started lecturing at the university. Marianne is bitter about it. "For us," she says, "it means that we can never have a holiday together and that your son works himself to death." As Borg sees it, Evald made a bargain. "And I know," he says smugly, "that Evald understands and respects me." Borg is stunned when Marianne replies: "That may be true, but he also hates you." At the end of the film, Borg tries to tell his son to forget the loan. But Evald misunderstands and insists that his father will get the money. The fact that Agda and Evald do not immediately respond to Borg's overtures helps save *Wild Strawberries* from sentimentality.

The warm relationship between Borg and Marianne, which has been developing throughout the film, reaches a climax when Marianne says goodnight to her father-in-law.

The two embrace each other fondly. "I like you, Marianne," says Borg; to which Marianne responds: "I like you too, Father Isak."

Wild Strawberries ends with another dream. Once more, we see the old summerhouse of Borg's childhood, the happy family, images shimmering with light. The first Sara appears. "Isak, darling," she says, "there are no wild strawberries left." Here, Borg is again telling himself that he has run out of time for life and love. "Aunt wants you to search for your father," Sara adds. "I will help you." Sara's love will enable Borg to find his father—that is, to be spiritually reborn. Finally, Borg sees his parents. His father is fishing, his mother is reading a book. They gaze at Borg across a body of water and laugh happily. Borg smiles back at them. In his "Tribute to Victor Sjöström," Bergman refers to the final close-ups of Borg smiling at his parents as indicating "clarity" and "reconciliation."[10]

Probably Borg's parents were never as they are pictured in the final dream. No matter. It is necessary for Borg to imagine this kind of relationship, for otherwise he might not be able to accept his fated end. At the conclusion of the film, Borg sees clearly the need to forgive his parents, to forgive himself, to accept life with its joys and sorrows, to make a renewed attempt to love others. By imagining a warm family life in the past, Borg makes it possible for himself to conceive of a better relationship with his own son, and thus prepares the way for a happy family life in Evald's union with Marianne.

The wild strawberries will bloom again.*

---

* In the prologue to *Wild Strawberries*, we see Borg writing the story of the film. Yet, in the prologue he still refers to himself as one who has withdrawn voluntarily from others, as one who has filled his life with work—in short, as one who seems to be still very much the same old Borg. Perhaps Bergman means by this to suggest that the new Borg is still struggling with the old Borg, that in spite of his recognition scenes he has not been immediately or completely changed. The fact that Borg could tell the truth about himself in his narration of the film shows his growth as a human being. There is no doubt that by the end of the film Bergman intends for us to believe in Borg's development. However, there is not a single clue to the narrator's alteration in the prologue. It is possible that Bergman sacrificed this detail in the interest of preserving suspense in the construction of his story.

8
The 400 Blows
1959

The French New Wave was a period in cinema when an emerging generation of film-makers rebelled against the established system. From 1959 to 1963, 170 young directors made their first feature picture. The term *politique des auteurs* (literally "the policy of authors") can be found in an essay entitled "*Une certaine tendance du cinema français*" by François Truffaut, which appeared in the *Cahiers du Cinema* of January 1954. It is commonly held that Truffaut's article represents the true beginning of the famous, and controversial, *auteur* theory. Actually, though, Truffaut merely put into clearer and simpler language ideas previously expressed by Jean-Luc Godard, Eric Rohmer, and Jacques Rivette. In his essay, Truffaut attacks a number of highly praised French pictures because, in his judgment, they are writer's creations. The true *auteur* (literally "author" or "creator"—however, for the *auteurists* the word is equivalent to "artist") of a film should be the director. But for that to be possible, Truffaut argues, the director has to be actively involved in scripting the film.

Over the years, Truffaut published numerous articles, film reviews, and interviews with directors, and in all of them he continued to develop his thesis. His chief aim was to provide the theoretical groundwork for a new kind of cinema: one in which directing would be seen not only as a personal means of visual expression but also as the projection of a specific Weltanschauung.* According to the original French *auteurists*, the proper conception of life—hence the proper subject for a film—involved the spiritual, psychological, and physical isolation of man in a corrupt modern society.

In practice, the New Wave film-makers did not all crank out the same kind of films. Techniques and themes varied greatly. Some directors overemphasized form. Others—like Truffaut—believed that both form and content were important. What they all had in common was a desire to make personal films. Of all Truffaut's films, the most personal—the most autobiographical—is *The 400 Blows*.

The plot of *The 400 Blows* (*Les Quatre Cent Coups*—a better rendering would be *Raising Hell*) revolves around Antoine Doinel (Jean-Pierre Léaud), aged twelve, whose basic problem is that no one loves him. Mme. Doinel (Claire Maurier), had conceived her son out of wedlock, had wanted an abortion, but had been talked into having her baby by her mother. Antoine's "father" (Albert Rémy) married his mother after she was already pregnant by another man. Antoine's best friend is René (Patrick Auffoy). The two boys, both of whom hate their strictly regimented school, play hookey. When asked why he was absent from class, Antoine says that his mother died. The parents come to school and M. Doinel slaps Antoine. Angry, hurt, and afraid, the boy reacts by running away from home and stealing. He is caught returning a typewriter he had taken from his father's office. Consequently, his parents turn him over to the courts. Antoine is sent to reform school, where the dehumanization of the classroom is carried further. One day, Antoine runs away to the sea, where he stops, feet in the water, waiting for the guards to take him back to the detention home. *Fin*.

Like Antoine, Truffaut ran away from home when he was

* In *Ecran Français* (1948), Alexander Astruc has written: "The cinema of today is capable of expressing any kind of reality . . . The film-maker/author writes with his camera as a writer writes with his pen" ("The Birth of a New *Avant-Garde: La Camera-Stylo*").

a boy. His father discovered him, pulled him along the street, and took him to the police station in Pigalle. From there Truffaut was taken in a police van, along with prostitutes, to the Center for Juvenile Delinquency at Villejuif. "It all happened exactly the way it happened in *The 400 Blows*," Truffaut has said (*The New York Times*, September 27, 1970). Unlike Antoine, Truffaut had a friend in André Bazin, the critic, who helped the future film artist by promising the authorities that if the youth was released he would get him a job.

According to Truffaut, when he cast for the part of Antoine in *The 400 Blows*, he was hoping to find an actor who bore a "moral resemblance," rather than a physical one, to the child he thought he had been.[1] Truffaut placed an ad in *France-Soir*, and sixty boys came to be interviewed and to receive a screen test. Since Jean-Pierre Léaud had adolescent problems himself, he seemed perfect for the part. Some people even said that the boy looked like Truffaut. The film-maker adapted the screenplay in certain respects to suit the actor, and he even allowed Léaud to improvise at least one important scene.

Although *The 400 Blows* is an autobiographical film, Truffaut was influenced by two works he admired. The first was Jean Vigo's 1933 classic *Zero for Conduct*, which also deals with adolescents who rebel against school authorities. There are many echoes of Vigo's film in *The 400 Blows*. The second influence was Roberto Rossellini's *Germany, Year Zero*, made in 1947. Both the Italian and French films have a gray, documentary, neo-realist look. Like Truffaut, Rossellini makes good use of a moving and panning camera. Unlike Truffaut, though, Rossellini has the boy in his film commit suicide.

Structurally, *The 400 Blows* is mainly vertical, although there is naturally some interest in how it will all end for young Antoine. Truffaut's chief concern is with character, mood, theme. The form is seriocomic. Both lyrical and documentary in approach, the tone is predominately humorous at the start, with an underlying sense of the boy's emotional pain; then, when M. Doinel turns Antoine over to the police, the mood grows increasingly somber, though still retaining comic touches. There is no pattern of sustained conflict, no plot in the causal sense. *The 400 Blows* is episodic, composed of many short scenes which tend to contrast with one another.

In general, the main contrast in the film is between images which suggest enclosure, imprisonment (the classroom, the Doinel flat, the detention home) and images which suggest freedom (Antoine and René playing hookey, Antoine's run to the sea). The tempo of the enclosure scenes tends to be slow, whereas the pace of the freedom scenes tends to be brisk. Psychologically, the clock seems not to move when we are unhappy; it appears to move in fast motion when we are enjoying ourselves. Of course, there is also contrast between the serious and comic aspects of the film. Sometimes Truffaut plays off his effects contrapuntally. Some scenes are funny and sad at the same time—such as when Antoine, frightened by his teacher, lies about his mother dying. There is contrast between the enchantment of Paris at night—the crowds of people, the brightly lighted shop windows, the gaiety and excitement—and the sight of Antoine being dragged by his father to the police station, or of Antoine riding in the police van. These scenes contain within themselves the basic form which structures the entire film.

Music in *The 400 Blows* is also a structural element. Although occasionally the mood of the music is "sad," most often the mood is "light," "jaunty," or "tinkly." During most of the film there is no music in the scenes which suggest imprisonment—such as in the classroom. When Antoine is alone in his flat, we hear music. It stops when his mother comes home from work. There is always music on the street, where Antoine and René are free. There is also music at home whenever Mme. Doinel shows her son a bit of love; when, for instance, she promises him a reward if he gets a good mark in French. There is also music at home when Antoine discovers Balzac, or when he lights a candle to Balzac. The one instance of music in the classroom is when Antoine unconsciously plagiarizes from Balzac in writing an essay. Truffaut's juxtaposition of music and silence suggest the two different worlds the boy inhabits.

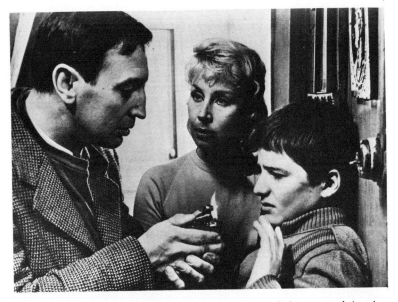

Antoine's "father" (Albert Remy) pushes a cigarette lighter toward Antoine (Jean-Pierre Leaud) as Mme. Doinel (Claire Maurier) watches. Antoine's candle burning in honor of Balzac started a fire in the apartment. "To collect insurance?" asks Doinel sarcastically. "You'll never make it with a candle, my boy. Do you want my lighter?"

Throughout the early part of the picture, Antoine is able to maintain a measure of freedom, which Jean Constantin's score accentuates. However, when M. Doinel drags Antoine to the police station, the boy's freedom disappears. Now we occassionally hear music in the imprisonment scenes. The music seems to be a haunting reminder of lost freedom. For example, music is played when Antoine is taken in the police van through the streets of Paris to the detention home. In the final scene of the film, though, the music again suggests freedom—although, unfortunately, it will be short-lived—when Antoine runs away from the detention home, races to the sea.

Normally, the term "subjective camera" means the use of the camera to simulate what a character sees. Truffaut believes that the subjective camera remains the antithesis of subjectivity. When the action is seen through the eyes of a character—that is to say, when the character, the camera, and the viewer all see the same thing—the audience does not really identify with the character. Truffaut gives no reason, however, for his position. Perhaps he believes that the subjective camera replaces the character with a mere perspective or look. There is no one there on the screen with whom we can identify. Whatever his reasons, Truffaut believes that film is truly subjective when the character's gaze encounters that of the viewer. An audience identifies with that character who is most frequently photographed in close-up.[2]

From beginning to end in *The 400 Blows*, the viewer identifies with Antoine. He is the character who is most often shot full on and in close-up. In the police van, Truffaut uses several kinds of subjective treatment. We see Antoine's face up close, a small tear of despair rolling down his cheek as he looks out at Paris through the bars. But we also see what he sees; the camera replaces him. And finally, we get a subjective angle, too. Truffaut places the camera just behind the boy's head, so that we see what he sees, but without the camera entirely supplanting him.

When Antoine talks to his mother, Truffaut several times has Léaud gaze directly into the camera. When Mme. Doinel replies to him, she too gazes at us. This type of shooting intensifies our sense of identification with the protagonist. When Mme. Doinel visits her son in the detention home, she is wearing a new hat. The boy stares at her across a table. Truffaut's camera tilts up from her face to her hat, and then tilts slowly down again. When Antoine's parents quarrel, Truffaut keeps his camera on the child's face for his reaction.

Antoine beds down on the floor in a sleeping bag. When his promiscuous mother comes home late at night, the camera is kept low. We do not see what Antoine sees, but our viewpoint remains at his level. Thus, when M. Doinel passes the sleeping bag in his pajamas, we see only his legs and Antoine in the background. Similarly, when Mme. Doinel enters the front door, we see only her silken legs as she tiptoes past her son.*

The most dramatic use of the subjective camera in the traditional sense occurs when Antoine takes a ride in "The Rotar"—a centrifuge or large wooden cylindrical drum at an amusement park. In this scene, Truffaut mixes objective shots of Antoine revolving in the drum with a subjective camera which shows us what the boy sees as the machine whirls around. The faces of the people watching "The Rotar" become a blur, as Antoine grows increasingly dizzy. Perhaps "The Rotar" is a visual trope for Antoine's chaotic existence.

Because Truffaut uses so many different kinds of subjective camera placement, we empathize fully with Antoine. When the tormented boy suddenly blurts out to his teacher that his mother died, the audience laughs nervously. Similarly, the viewer recoils when M. Doinel slaps Antoine for lying about his mother's death, or when Antoine is again slapped in the face—by a detention home attendant—for eating before a whistle had blown.

As suggested earlier in another context, we become so immersed in Antoine's character that we experience time as he experiences it. When the boy runs away from home, he steals a bottle of milk. Truffaut patiently allows us to watch the starving

* Unfortunately, this scene does not appear in one print of *The 400 Blows*. Truffaut has made numerous revisions of his film since 1959.

child swallow down the entire bottle. Likewise, when Antoine rolls a cigarette at the detention home, Truffaut lets the "action" happen in real time. The intensity derived from our close involvement with Antoine—from the various uses of camera subjectivity, and from the psychological uses of time— gives *The 400 Blows* a powerful realistic effect.

Truffaut's film is thoroughly cinematic—it could not be done in any other form. It achieves universality not only because of its theme, but also because of its treatment. There are many scenes in which there is no dialogue at all—such as when Antoine and René play hookey, or when Antoine escapes from the detention home. One might almost say that *The 400 Blows* is a half-silent movie.

Truffaut sets up a satisfying aesthetic tension by alternating static camera shots with a moving camera. The most outstanding example of a stationary camera in the film is a scene in which Antoine has an interview with a female psychologist. Truffaut keeps his camera steadily on Antoine, dissolving from one shot to another to indicate a passage of time, and never showing the face of the woman whose questions we hear on the sound track. (This scene was improvised by Jean-Pierre Léaud.)

Yet, as noted, there is much variety in the visuals. In the course of one scene, Truffaut will pan back and forth between characters, even occasionally swish pan. He will dazzle the viewer with various camera angles. Nevertheless, we never get the feeling that the film-maker is showing off, or simply playing with his camera. The manner of shooting is perfectly expressive of the mood, the motivation in the scene. The many panning shots, for example, create a sense of flow, a lyrical continuity. When Antoine catches his first glimpse of the sea there is a long slow pan from right to left—as though from the boy's point of view—along the shoreline. But when Truffaut comes to the end of the pan, Antoine is discovered at the left of the screen, running again. The panning shot flows smoothly into Antoine's movement. What was subjective becomes objective.

A guard hands Antoine a cup of coffee through his cell door at the detention home.

TEN FILM CLASSICS: A RE-VIEWING

As Alexander Astruc points out, the film-maker as author "writes with his camera as a writer writes with his pen." In the first scene of the film, Antoine is not allowed out to recess with the rest of his class. Truffaut crosscuts between Antoine alone in the classroom and the other children frolicking in the school-yard. With his camera, the *auteur* is "saying": Look how isolated Antoine is from everyone. And this feeling of isolation attaches to the boy throughout the film.

Similarly, Truffaut's technique shows us that there is no love in the Doinel family. He keeps his camera in tight on the father and mother and son in their cramped flat. But this type of shooting does not suggest family solidarity, because the close-ups reveal little or no warmth of facial expression. These people are bunched together out of economic necessity. The photography "says" that the Doinels are frustrated and unhappy.

Later in the film, Truffaut shoots Antoine through the bars of his cell in the police station, and later still through the bars of the police van. These shots tell us everything we need to know about the boy's situation.

Sometimes Truffaut uses a sign within the film to comment ironically on the action. For example, as the students leave school, the camera reveals some words above the school entrance: "Liberty—Equality—Fraternity." When Antoine runs away from home and is alone on the city streets, he passes a shop window with a decoration on the glass: "Merry Christmas." Occasionally Truffaut, like other New Wave directors, indulges himself. When a gym teacher takes his class for a jog on the streets, the camera at one point lingers on a name painted across a wall: "Giraudoux"—the French novelist and playwright much admired by the New Wave film-makers.*

The ending of *The 400 Blows* is one of the most celebrated sequences in the history of film and the final shot one of the most memorable. At the detention home, the boys are playing

---

* When the Doinels go to the movies, they see *Paris Belongs to Us* (1958–60), the first film of Jacques Rivette, the *Cahiers du Cinema* critic. Truffaut was co-producer of the Rivette film.

soccer. Suddenly Antoine dashes off the field, darts to a fence, slips through a hole in the bottom of the fence—and runs away. Whistles blow. One guard pursues Antoine. Now Truffaut shows his visual mastery. As Antoine runs . . . and runs . . . and runs, the camera tracks alongside of him in one long continuous take. The boy runs past farmhouses, open fields, hedges, empty buildings—but never past any people. He is completely alone.

Dissolve. Antoine, still running, slips down the side of a hill. Here he sees the sea, and here Truffaut pans the length of it, in the shot which was described previously. Descending a large open stairway, Antoine rushes toward the beach. The camera moves with the boy. Finally, he reaches the sea. He steps into it, the water swirling around his ankles. For a moment, the viewer wonders whether Antoine is going to commit suicide. But no—suddenly he turns and walks in the surf alongside the shore, and then steps back on the beach. The camera dollies in on Antoine—and suddenly the shot freezes into a still. All motion, finally, ceases. Antoine is trapped, his gaze meeting ours.

The juxtaposition of the static interview between Antoine and his mother at the detention home with the following sequence involving the protracted traveling shot as Antoine attempts his escape is visually striking. But even this arresting camera work is dwarfed by the inspired conclusion. As the camera tracks in on Antoine, he stares directly at the viewer. It is impossible for us to escape involvement in his fate. There is something mysterious about his expression in that final close-up. For some viewers, Antoine seems to be gazing at them accusingly. Others see him as sad, frustrated, questioning. And still others regard the boy's expression as merely impassive. The freeze frame which ends the film is similarly ambiguous. Does it simply put off the determination of the boy's problem? Or does it, on the contrary, suggest the unchanging nature of the boy's future—his ruined life? One thing is sure. That face will haunt us forever.

Thematically, Truffaut is "saying" in *The 400 Blows* that adolescence is a painful time of life. This belief was his first impulse for making the film. Passing from childhood to adulthood, Antoine is treated in contradictory ways. He is punished in school for looking at a picture of a girl in a bathing suit, but when the candle he has lighted in honor of Balzac starts a fire at home, he is rewarded by being taken to the movies by his parents. Mme. Doinel criticizes Antoine for stealing—yet she cheats on her husband and at least on one occasion steals money from her son.

Mme. Doinel resents having Antoine around. His birth forced her to marry a man she obviously does not love. Antoine's mere existence annoys her. He is a symbol of her bondage and a reminder that she is growing older. (In the first scene at home, we see Mme. Doinel gaze at herself in a mirror, smoothing the lines of her skin.) M. Doinel is kinder to Antoine than Mme. Doinel, but he remains basically indifferent to the boy. When the father tells the mother that her cousin is having her fourth child in three years, Mme. Doinel exclaims: "Like rabbits . . . disgusting"; to which M. Doinel immediately remarks: "Apropos, what are we going to do about the kid's vacation?" Mme. Doinel says that vacation time is still eight months away. "You can't plan too early for vacations," M. Doinel says. For him, too, Antoine is a burden.

In spite of its apparent simplicity, however, *The 400 Blows* is not without its social criticism. The film is no mere psychological study. As Truffaut sees it, French schools crush the spontaneity of children through physical and verbal abuse, and through education by rote. The schoolroom—which resembles the police station and the detention home—turns out either robots or rebels. The family merely reflects the condition of the large society outside the home. Sometimes Truffaut links the two spheres dramatically. In the first part of the film, M. Doinel shocks the viewer by suddenly slapping Antoine's face because he lied about his mother dying. In the second part of the film, an attendant at the detention home similarly shocks the viewer by slapping Antoine's face for eating prematurely. There is no love at home, or in the schoolroom, or anywhere else.

Thus far, Truffaut has made three other films featuring Jean-Pierre Léaud as Antoine: an episode entitled "Antoine and Colette" in *Love at Twenty* (1962), *Stolen Kisses* (1968), and *Bed and Board* (1970). None of these later works has the impact of *The 400 Blows*. In each succeeding film, Truffaut has made Antoine adjust himself more and more to society. Pauline Kael, reviewing *Stolen Kisses*, has observed: "Truffaut has made [Antoine] so healthy that I can't believe that that sensitive boy could have become so *trivially* healthy. The child's desperation has disappeared, and the adult world is now a collection of harmless eccentrics, some of them unfortunate but most of them—well, lovable."[3] Has Truffaut finally retired Antoine from the screen?

Perhaps not. When Truffaut was in America to plug *Day for Night* (1973), he told an interviewer that he might one day bring Antoine back again. "I'm thinking about putting him in a situation with a psychiatrist," Truffaut said. "Antoine would tell him all the things I've done with him" (*The New York Times*, October 9, 1973). No matter how Truffaut may have mishandled Antoine over the years, nothing can ever erase the achievement of *The 400 Blows*.*

* Truffaut has said: "When I see [*The 400 Blows*] again now, I . . . find it rather awkward, but the required effects were often very simple ones and it's a film which makes me feel very nostalgic. I get the feeling I'll never again find such a direct subject. There were things in it about which I felt so deeply that I had no choice, there was only one way to shoot them. What's more, now that I tend to produce more refined work (I am not using the word in a flattering sense, in fact I don't find it a step forward), I yearn for simple effects which are able to move everyone at the same time—I am very sensitive to the collective spectacle."[4]

9
L'Avventura
1960

Like Fellini, Michelangelo Antonioni set out to extend the limits of neo-realism. After World War II, the neo-realists saw poverty as the chief problem facing Italian society; human solidarity, it was felt, would bring about the necessary changes in the economic and political structure. But as Antonioni views it, the main difficulty has become precisely the *lack* of human solidarity. Not poverty—but alienation, inability to communicate, and boredom are the real problems. Because modern man is spiritually empty, because—according to Antonioni—God is dead and the old moral code obsolete, we see a symptomatic obsessive sexuality everywhere. "Our time is one in which it seems to me there is a decadence of love," Antonioni has said. "The very quality of emotion has changed . . . Eros is sick."[1]

Stylistically, every Antonioni film has his distinctive "signature" on it. He has little tolerance for plot, or linear progression, or causal structural relationships. To him, such concerns reveal a mechanical or artificial approach to film form. Antonioni is interested, not in physical action, not in drama, but in the inner lives of his characters, in their ambience, in mood. Because of his concentration on the psychology of his characters, the tempo of an Antonioni film is closer to real time than the average film, in which there is much more condensation. His scenes tend to be protracted, deliberately torpid, slow-moving.

Visually, Antonioni likes to present a scene devoid of people—sometimes before they enter, or after they leave. "If there is any one thing I do often," the film-maker has remarked, "it is to focus on inanimate objects instead of people to reduce things to an abstraction and demonstrate the lack of feeling in people" (*New York Times*, January 1, 1967). A typical Antonioni shot will show two characters talking, but without looking at each other. This kind of composition obviously underlines the lack of communication between people which is one of the director's themes. Although the pace of an Antonioni scene resembles life itself, and hence seems "objective," his *mise-en-scène* is extremely stylized. As a boy, Antonioni ws interested in designing architectural models; as a film-maker, he uses buildings, open areas, and landscapes to reflect the emotional quality of a character at a certain moment. An Antonioni scene often has a staged, choreographed look. Fellini has observed: "[Antonioni] has the eye of a photographer. His talent is in the eye, not in the blood . . . The allure of his pictures is very exterior and very elegant. They have a strange result, like *Vogue:* sophisticated but cold."[2] Consequently, Antonioni rarely employs a subjective camera (that is, a shot simulating what a character sees), because that way we would tend to identify more strongly with his people. Instead, Antonioni will use a subjective angle (that is, a shot in which part of the character witnessing an event remains visible on the screen), so that a certain aloofness is maintained on the part of both the film-maker and the viewer.

We get to know an Antonioni character only gradually in the course of a film, sometimes in a seemingly incidental, almost offhand manner. Exposition—which traditionally comes at the beginning of a drama or narrative—often comes around the middle, or even later, in an Antonioni film. In short, we get to know his characters the way we get to know people in real life—bit by bit. There is always some mystery surrounding Antonioni's characters; we are given less cues than is normally the case in film as to how we should interpret and evaluate them. Even Antonioni claims not to know the answers to certain questions about his characters.

Because "Less is more" remains Antonioni's working

aesthetic, he uses music sparingly in his films. He prefers to let the picture "say" what he has to impart to the viewer. Nevertheless, he does on occasion employ music in support of the image; it is always used to complement the visual. The same is true of Antonioni's orchestration of sound effects. Natural sounds—such as the whir of a motorboat or the slapping of waves against rocks—add immeasurably to what we see on the screen. As Antonioni has put it: "the images cannot stand alone, without these sounds, just as those sounds would have no meaning at all if they were detached from the images."[3] Like all great directors, Antonioni also knows how to play off silence and sound effectively.

Now that we have made some generalizations about Antonioni's art, let us turn to a consideration of his masterpiece, *L'Avventura* (*The Adventure*).

The film opens with a long shot of Anna (Lea Massari), a brunette in her mid-twenties, walking across the courtyard of a villa. Her father (Renzo Ricci), a wealthy retired diplomat, is talking to a worker. Anna's father is lamenting the fact that soon this section will be filled with new but cheap residential housing. Immediately Antonioni has announced one of the main themes of his film: the past, and with it traditional values, is vanishing; a new world is coming into being—a world which will demand altered moral attitudes to keep pace with the changes science and technology are making.

Anna informs her father that she is going away for several days on a yachting trip. "Don't they still wear sailors' caps with the name of the yacht on them?" he asks; to which Anna replies: "Not anymore." Again, Antonioni touches on the theme of change. During this scene, father and daughter scarcely glance at each other. "That kind will never marry you, my child," the father says. "Up till now," Anna tells him, "I've been the one who won't marry him." In this exchange, Antonioni prepares us for Anna's ennui, her spiritual emptiness.

Claudia (Monica Vitti), a young woman with blonde hair, appears. The two friends get into Anna's car and the chauffeur drives off. When they arrive in front of a palazzo, Anna heads for a bar. Claudia is astonished. "If I had a man waiting for me for half an hour and whom I hadn't seen for a month—"; but Anna checks her by saying: "I could just as well go without seeing him today." And she goes on to explain that, whereas separation from Sandro allows her to daydream about him, being in his presence obliges her to communicate with him, which she finds difficult to do. Nevertheless, she goes upstairs to see him, leaving Claudia to wait below.

Sandro (Gabriele Ferzetti), who is about forty, seems pleased to see Anna, but she keeps staring at him in a strange way. "Well, what's wrong?" he asks. Anna begins to undress. "But your friend is waiting downstairs," he objects. "Let her wait," replies Anna. And they go to bed together. It is clear that sex is the only way in which Anna feels she can be intimate with Sandro. Yet, in spite of the apparent hunger she displays in taking the initiative, Anna obviously feels nothing. The "lovemaking" remains cold and mechanical.

Next the scene moves to the yacht. Here we are introduced to the boating party: Raimondo (Lelio Luttazzi), a man in his thirties; Corrado (James Addams), an older man; Giulia (Dominique Blanchar), a woman in her late thirties; and Patrizia (Esmeralda Ruspoli), a woman of about forty. Out at sea, Antonioni uses the surroundings to make a statement about the emotional aridity of his characters. As the yacht slips along the coast of an island, Giulia observes that all the islands in the vicinity were once volcanoes. There is no life in the volcanoes now, just as there is no life in the characters. Anna goes for a swim. While she is in the water, she screams: "Oh, a shark!" Everyone is concerned. Sandro helps her out of the water and back onto the yacht. Later, however, we find out that there was no shark in the water. Anna cried shark just for a "joke," simply as a release from boredom.

Medium shot of Anna and Claudia alone in a cabin on the yacht. Anna shows her friend two blouses. "Which one should I wear?" she asks. Claudia selects a dark one. Anna insists that Claudia try it on. "It looks better on you than me," she says.

"Keep it." This scene is important in the development of Antonioni's theme, though it appears to be inconsequential at the time it is played.

The yachting party decide to visit one of the islands. Antonioni focuses on a scene between Anna and Sandro, as the couple discuss the nature of their relationship. Surrounded by bleak, jagged rocks, the sound of waves washing relentlessly nearby, Anna tells Sandro: "The thought of losing you makes me want to die. And yet—I don't feel you anymore." Sandro obtusely misunderstands what she is trying to communicate to him. "Not even yesterday, at my house?" he responds. "You didn't feel me then?" Antonioni dissolves to the next scene.

When it is time for the party to leave the island, Anna is missing. No one knows what has happened to her. Indeed, Antonioni himself confesses that he does not know where Anna has gone—whether she had accidentally drowned, committed suicide, run off, or been kidnapped. We never see her again in the film.

The search for Anna on the island is very long, because Antonioni wishes to show his characters' alienation from nature, from the past, from each other, and from themselves. The characters seem not to belong on the island; they are an incongruous sight, dwarfed by sky and rocks and sea. At one point, Raimondo discovers an ancient vase. "There's an entire city buried beneath us, " he says. And then, clumsily, he drops the vase, smashing it on the rocks. Symbolically, the film-maker is suggesting that these characters have been disconnected from a sense of historical continuity; they are unable to make contact with a usable past. Sandro is less concerned over Anna than over Anna's feelings about him. "Did she ever talk to you about me?" he asks Claudia. Soon the characters grow bored with the search for the perverse Anna. They wish to leave the island. It is plain that these aristocrats have lost touch with their own humanity—they are short on understanding, tenderness, compassion.

Anna's father—notified of her disappearance—comes to the island. Claudia shows him two books she discovered in his daughter's suitcase; the Bible and F. Scott Fitzgerald's novel

Tender Is the Night. As Anna's father sees it, no one who reads the bible would commit the sin of self-destruction. Fitzgerald remains one of Antonioni's favorite novelists. Like the American writer, the Italian film-maker is both attracted to the rich and repelled by them. In the original version of *Tender Is the Night*, which starts out by focusing on a group of rich people on the French Riviera, a young woman named Rosemary Hoyt seems to be the main character but gradually recedes in importance, giving way to the real center of interest, Dick Diver. Antonioni has imitated Fitzgerald here—and elsewhere (as we shall see).

Throughout the search sequence on the island, Antonioni makes us aware of a growing attraction between Sandro and Claudia. Everything in the modern world is impermanent—this note was struck at the beginning of the film when Anna's father sadly reflected on the cheap new housing going up around him. The same theme appears everywhere in *L'Avventura*. Like the industrial, technological social structures around them, the emotions of the characters in the film are also impermanent. Back on the yacht, alone with Claudia in a cabin, Sandro reaches for his fiancée's best friend and kisses her. In spite of herself, Claudia responds. Then, shocked at herself, she breaks free and runs upstairs to the deck. During this scene, Claudia is wearing the dark blouse Anna had given her. Antonioni seems to be saying that in a consumer society, one in which depersonalization and dehumanization are rampant, people are as disposable and as replaceable as paper drinking cups.

Shot of Claudia, seated in the waiting room of a train station. She is going to the villa of the Princess Montalto. Although Claudia is attracted to Sandro, and although she is going to the Montaltos for a "good time," she nevertheless remains the one consistently sympathetic character in *L'Avventura*. Claudia is genuinely concerned over Anna, and just as genuinely appalled by her own desire for Sandro. Later in the film, we learn that Claudia is not a member of the upper class. She was born poor, but somehow she has managed to attach herself to the aristocracy. Sandro enters the train station and tries to persuade Claudia to stay with him. She refuses.

Once Claudia is in her compartment on the train, however,

she discovers that Sandro has followed her. Again, he seeks to persuade her to stay with him. In a skillful use of contrapuntal structure, Antonioni plays off Sandro's attempt to seduce Claudia against the dialogue in the next compartment in which a boy is making advances towards a girl.

> *Boy:* I'm telling you—my friend knows you and has told me about you.
> *Girl:* Does she work in Catania?
> *Boy:* Yes, she's a gardener.
> *Girl:* Then it isn't possible for her to know me. In the villa where I work, the gardener is a man.
> *Boy:* That doesn't prove anything. Since they are both gardeners, they spoke to one another about you.
> *Girl:* What did they say about me?
> *Boy:* That you were a nice girl, and that you always mind your own business.

Antonioni's counterpoint technique here is strikingly similar to a scene in *Tender Is the Night*. When Nicole contemplates abandoning Dick, her husband, and taking a lover, she struggles with herself in her garden:

> [Nicole] was somewhat shocked at the thought of being interested in another man—but other women have lovers— why not me? In the fine spring morning the inhibitions of the male world disappeared and she reasoned gaily as a flower . . . Through a cluster of boughs she saw two men carrying rakes and spades and talking in a counterpoint of Niçoise and Provençal. Attracted by their words and gestures she caught the sense:
> "I laid her down here."
> "I took her behind the vines there."
> "She doesn't care—neither does he . . ."
> "Well, I laid her down here—"
> . . . .
> "Well, I don't care where you laid her down. Until that night I never even felt a woman's breast against my chest since I was married—twelve years ago." Nicole watched them through the boughs; it seemed all right what they were saying—one thing was good for one person, another for another.[4]

L'Avventura 1960

Now that Anna has disappeared, Sandro (Gabriele Ferzetti) seeks to persuade Claudia (Monica Vitti) to become his new love, in *L'Avventura*.

141

TEN FILM CLASSICS: A RE-VIEWING

In both *L'Avventura* and *Tender Is the Night*, a young woman is engaged in an inner conflict between passion and loyalty; while she struggles with herself, a second scene is enacted, which crudely comments on the woman's eventual surrender to sexuality. Antonioni even borrows the small detail about the "gardeners" from Fitzgerald's novel. In *L'Avventura*, however, Claudia temporarily resists Sandro's appeal and he angrily gets off the train.

Next we discover Sandro in Messina, looking for a journalist who might have some information about Anna. It turns out that he does not. While he is in Messina, though, Sandro sees an American young woman named Gloria Perkins (Dorothy De Polioli), who has attracted a noisy crowd because of her sex appeal. Her dress is so tight that the seam of her skirt has split. The journalist tells Sandro that Gloria Perkins is available for anyone with fifty thousand lira. Later in the film, Sandro will become involved with Gloria Perkins. The horde of men lusting after this woman reveals Antonioni's theme of overemphasis on sex as a means of filling a spiritual void in life.

The scene shifts to the Montalto villa, where we find the yachting party mingling with other rich people. Corrado tells the princess: "Why don't you sell this villa. I could convert it into a nice clinic for people suffering from nervous breakdowns." (In *Tender Is the Night* Nicole's family buys Dick, who is a psychiatrist, a clinic in which to treat sick members of the upper class.) Claudia, still upset over Anna's disappearance and still thinking about Sandro, goes to Patrizia's room. There is a black wig in the room, and Claudia tries it on. She looks like Anna. Unconsciously, Claudia wishes to solve her inner conflict by becoming Anna and thus alleviating her sense of guilt for desiring Sandro.

Claudia accompanies Giulia to the room of Goffredo (Giovanni Petrucci), a young painter of nudes. He tries to coax Giulia into posing for him. After a brief resistance, the woman submits to the boy's kisses and Claudia, disturbed by what she sees, exits. Going downstairs, however, she pauses before a mirror and smooths her hair. It is clear that the more loose

142

sexuality Claudia perceives, the weaker her own resistance will grow in respect to Sandro.

A druggist has been quoted in a newspaper as saying that a woman matching Anna's description had bought tranquilizers from him. Sandro and Claudia start out from different direc- . tions to question the man. When Sandro arrives, however, he can learn little from the druggist—who, according to his bitter wife of three months, mentally undresses every woman he sees. Like most of the characters in *L'Avventura*, the druggist suffers from a sick erotic impulse. He claims, though, to have seen Anna board a bus to Noto. Removing Claudia's bags from her chauffeur-driven car, Sandro puts them in his convertible. At last, Sandro and Claudia are together.

The couple arrive at Noto, a modern town: white, cold-looking, impersonal architecture—completely devoid of people. "This isn't a town," says Claudia. "It's a cemetery." In a long shot, we see Claudia and Sandro drive off out of the frame. For a long time, Antonioni holds the shot on the empty town.— Then there is an abrupt cut to a close-up of Claudia, an ecstatic expression on her face, her arms around Sandro, the open sky behind her. They are making love on the grass, outside of town. Fully dressed, they roll on the ground together, kissing both tenderly and passionately. The juxtaposition of the long shot of the empty Noto with the close-up of Claudia suggests that the lovemaking is a response to the dismal feeling engendered in them by a sterile modern existence. Suddenly a freight train passes, startling the lovers. This symbol of modern industrial society calls the lovers back to reality: it is a mechanical snake in the garden.

Back in Noto, Sandro goes into the House Trinacria to see if Anna has registered there. Claudia waits on the street because she feels too guilty to meet Anna, should Sandro locate her. On the street, however, scores of men stare at Claudia as though she were an object to be consumed, as though she were another Gloria Perkins. Finally, frightened and ashamed, she takes refuge in a paint store until Sandro joins her.

The couple are led by a nun to a church roof, overlooking

he piazza of Noto, which is in the baroque style opposed to the modernistic design of the rest of the town. Here we learn that Sandro started out to be an architect but settled into being an estimator for Ettore, a builder, because there was more money in it. He would like to become an architect again, and Claudia encourages him: "I'm sure you could make beautiful things." Sandro, who will never of course go back to being creative, remarks: "Who needs beautiful things now? How long will they last? Once they had centuries of life before them. Now—ten, twenty years at the most." Then, suddenly, the depressed Sandro asks Claudia to marry him. She is astonished. It is clear that the man is reaching out for the woman as a cripple would reach out for a crutch. Sandro would like to return to the womb, hide from his problems, blot them out with sex.

In their dingy hotel room, Claudia—who is obviously pleased that Sandro wants to marry her, though she is not ready for it yet—does a playful dance around him to the accompaniment of music from a van with a loud-speaker below. Sandro wants to go for a walk, but Claudia is still dressing. She half pretends that she cannot live without him for a moment. "You must tell me that you want to kiss my shadow on the wall," she says.* Finally, Sandro manages to leave. It is obvious that he is depressed, that he does not share Claudia's joyous mood.

Sandro walks to the museum to recapture his youthful enthusiasm, but is irritated to find that the place is closed. Then he sees a young architect who is working on an ink drawing—working in a way which is a reproach to the older man. In a fit of jealousy, Sandro ruins the sketch by spilling the bottle of ink over it. A fist fight almost develops. Shot of schoolboys in black uniforms, accompanied by priests in black filing out of a church. Sandro follows them, his light suit contrasting with their black garb. Here, Antonioni appears to be "saying" that Sandro's

---

* Sandro gives up being a architect, just as Dick in *Tender is the Night* stops taking his profession seriously. Both men sell out for money. And both men turn to women as a means of escape from themselves: "[Dick] was in love with every pretty woman he saw now, their forms at a distance, their shadows on a wall."[5] Compare this statement with Claudia's line above.

High angle shot of Claudia lying on the floor.

emptiness is related to the loss of faith, the breakdown of the Christian world view, and the emergence of modern capitalistic society.

Returning to the hotel, still angry and depressed, Sandro tries to make love to Claudia. His approach is crude and direct, and the young woman refuses. It is apparent to the viewer—and Claudia probably senses this—that Sandro wants to use her as a substitute gratification for the void in his life, for his lost opportunities, and for his inability to reverse his drift toward self-destruction. Claudia persuades Sandro that they must continue their search for Anna.

Instead, however, Sandro and Claudis appear at an elegant hotel in Taormina, where we subsequently discover members of the yachting party as well as some characters who were at the Montalto villa. It would seem that Claudia and Sandro are now playing the same stultifying game previously played by Anna and Sandro.

A clerk shows Sandro and Claudia to their room. After the clerk leaves, Sandro makes fun of him. "A robot would do just as well," he says. The irony here is that Sandro himself acts like a robot—all of his behavior, including his compulsive love-making, is mechanical. "Do you know that when I was a boy I wanted to be a diplomat?" he tells Claudia. "Strange, but I never saw myself as rich. Instead, I imagined myself a genius, living in a furnished room someplace. Now, I have two houses. And as for being a genius—well, I never got into the habit." In this scene, it is plain that Sandro will never leave Ettore. Sandro is like a machine, unable to make a creative alteration in the direction his life has taken.

Sandro leaves Claudia, who wants to sleep, and goes downstairs where a small orchestra is playing for a room filled with people. Here, Sandro encounters Gloria Perkins again. Antonioni cuts back to Claudia's room, where we see her stirring restlessly in bed . . . Daybreak—and Claudia, fully dressed now, goes to Patrizia's room. Since Sandro has not returned as yet, she is afraid that Anna has come back, that she has lost him. At first, she confesses, the thought of Anna's death saddened her immensely. Now the thought that Anna might be alive frightens her.

Leaving Patrizia, Claudia searches for Sandro through the corridors and lounge and various rooms of the hotel. In a huge dining room, she discovers Sandro making love to Gloria Perkins on a couch. Claudia is shocked. She runs off, and Sandro struggles to his feet. "Aren't you going to leave me a souvenir?" asks Gloria. Disgusted with himself, Sandro throws some money down on the couch, between the woman's legs. Gloria scoops up the bills with her feet. Antonioni's shot of the money between Gloria's legs is a telling and symbolic commentary on the nature of Sandro's relationship with her.

The last scene of the film takes place in an open square. There is a bench, an iron railing, a dilapidated church with a bell tower beyond the railing. Claudia, weeping, watches trees bending against the morning wind. As she leans against the railing, Sandro crosses the piazza, walking in a stiff, robot-like way. He sits down on the bench. Claudia stands behind him. As Sandro begins to weep, Claudia hesitantly begins to caress the back of his head. Long shot of Claudia standing behind Sandro, her hand on his head, a concrete wall beyond the railing on the right hand side of the screen, a glimpse of Mount Etna in the distance on the left hand side of the screen. Fade out . . .

Claudia had deceived herself that she and Sandro loved each other—at the end she knows better. Sandro is the mere semblance of a man, unable to love anyone, incapable of rising above the empty pursuit of money and sensual pleasure. He weeps for the soul he has lost, the illusions which will never come again, for his helplessness. As for Claudia, all she can feel now for Sandro is pity.

Antonioni has said that the composition of the last shot is highly symbolic, with the frame divided in half. The wall represents Sandro and pessimism; the mountain stands for Claudia and optimism. The film-maker will not admit that Sandro is doomed—there is always hope, he thinks. One thing is certain. Claudia has forgiven Sandro; she will not leave him. The reason for this, according to Antonioni, is that Claudia knows she resembles Sandro: she had betrayed Anna as Sandro has betrayed her. As Antonioni sees it, Claudia's sense of pity for Sandro remains positive and humane—the one hope for a better future, not only for Claudia and Sandro, but also for the human race.[6]

10
Bonnie and Clyde
1967

The script for *Bonnie and Clyde* was written by Robert Benton and David Newman, who got the idea for the film from reading John Toland's book *The Dillinger Days* (1963), which has a chapter on the real Bonnie and Clyde. In writing the scenario, their first, they were influenced by the seriocomic structuring of Truffaut's *Shoot the Piano Player* (1960) and *Jules and Jim* (1961). Benton and Newman wanted Truffaut to direct the film, but arrangements with the French film-maker couldn't be worked out. Consequently, Arthur Penn became the director of *Bonnie and Clyde*.

Penn, who had directed *The Left-handed Gun* (1957) and *The Miracle Worker* (1962), is of two minds about the authorship of *Bonnie and Clyde*. He has often stated that, in spite of changes he made in the script, the film is basically the screenwriters' creation. Yet Penn has also declared: "There is only one event in making movies, and that's the director's event . . . I don't care how well-written the script is. You can get into a motel room in Texas, and the dialogue can be exquisite, but what you choose to look at and how you look at it is everything."[1] Actually, credit for the enormous success of *Bonnie and Clyde* should be distributed among everyone concerned in the enterprise—not only the scenarists and the director, but also the actors, the cinematographer, Burnett Guffey, and the film editor, Dede Allen, should receive special mention. Like *Citizen Kane* and *On the Waterfront*, *Bonnie and Clyde* represents a triumph of collaborative American film-making.

Click, and the story of Bonnie and Clyde begins.

The film opens in black-and-white. We see a series of biographical police cards—short, impersonal notations about the title characters— and snapshots of the Clyde Barrow and Bonnie Parker families. Between the police cards and the photographs the credits appear, the lettering of which turn symbolically from white to blood-red. At first the sound track is quiet—except for the steady, ominous click of an old-fashioned camera shutter. Then, halfway through the credits, we hear the sound of Rudy Vallee crooning *Deep Night*, a popular love song of the thirties.

The introduction to *Bonnie and Clyde* arouses a complicated response in the viewer. Coming from what appears to be a long way off, Vallee's voice invites us to journey backward in time nostalgically. But other elements of the opening destroy this too comfortable attitude on our part. There is an impression of something about to happen, something terrible, in the relentless click, click, click of the camera—which sounds like a gun—and in the sight of the faded snapshots rapidly displacing each other in a blurred fashion. Without consciously realizing it, we become involved in the "is-ness" of what we see and hear. Whatever happens up there on the screen—we will be a part of it.

Dissolve to a tight close-up of a woman's bright red lips. Abruptly Penn pulls back his camera to expose Bonnie (Faye Dunaway) naked except for bikini underpants in her cramped, shabby room in West Dallas, Texas. The young woman's beautiful face remains a study in boredom and romantic longing. As presented in the film, Bonnie Parker is a kind of Emma Bovary—a narcissistic mediocre poet and a discontented waitress who is obliged to dodge the embraces of truckdrivers in a greasy cafe as she envisions a greener world beyond the Dust Bowl. In order to emphasize Bonnie's feelings of entrapment, Penn keeps his camera in close to her—shooting her at one point through the bars of the bed she is lying on—tracking with her as she moves across the room.

Downstairs appears Clyde (Warren Beatty), wearing a dark suit and a white panama hat. He is planning to steal Mrs.

Bonnie and Clyde 1967

Parker's automobile. Framed half-naked in the window, Bonnie harangues him. After hurriedly slipping into a cheap lightweight dress, she clatters noisily down the rickety wooden outside staircase in order to confront the would-be thief. As she does so, Penn shoots her from a low angle. The glare of the sun above the roof and the shadows on the side of the house, however, prevent the viewer from seeing up the woman's skirt. Throughout this sequence, the audience cannot forget the promise of Bonnie's lovely body—a body which is teasingly never shown in its complete nakedness. The onlooker is convinced that Bonnie and Clyde are going to enjoy (and the spectator vicariously) intense sexual gratification. Yet, the sight of Bonnie as she descends the staircase—her shoes thumping on the steps, her figure grotesquely foreshortened thanks to the camera angle—prepares the viewer for a comic reversal of expectations.

After a few words with Bonnie, Clyde changes his mind about stealing Mrs. Parker's car. Instead, he decides to walk Bonnie to the cafe where she works. As they banter with each other on the hot empty street, Bonnie becomes increasingly fascinated by the seemingly virile young man. Clyde's limp, however, suggests that he is neither physically nor psychologically whole. While in prison, Bonnie learns, he chopped two toes off his right foot in order to escape work.

The couple stop to drink Cokes. Again, Penn keeps his camera in tight on the two characters, so that we feel the attraction growing between them. Except for his limp, Clyde continues to project a forceful image. At one point the camera reveals Clyde's face close up from a low angle, a Coke bottle slanting from one side of his mouth, a wooden matchstick from the other. As Clyde shows Bonnie his gun, he wiggles the matchstick suggestively. A close-up of the weapon at the level of Clyde's crotch, followed by a reaction shot of Bonnie touching the barrel with awe, leaves no doubt in the viewer's mind on the score of symbolism. Sex and violence thus become linked at the outset of the picture.

Bonnie taunts Clyde into using his gun. "All right," he responds. "You just wait right here and keep your eyes open."

Across the street is Ritts Groceries. Clyde goes into the store. With a camera positioned just behind Bonnie, we see the storefront from a subjective angle. Presently Clyde emerges from the doorway, walking backwards, his gun pointed at someone inside. Then he turns, grins and shows Bonnie a handful of bills. Firing a warning shot in the air, Clyde takes Bonnie's hand and they run down the street together.

The couple are on their way.

And as their stolen automobile roars off, Bonnie and Clyde finally introduce themselves. Crime seems to be a mode of self-realization, a way of achieving identity. That the two young people are self-deceived, however, is made clear throughout the film. *Bonnie and Clyde* is less concerned with the period of the Great Depression than with man's continuing search for meaning in a society bereft of worthwhile goals and values. Like so many people today, Bonnie and Clyde know neither *what* they are nor *who* they are. Existentially, violence becomes a way of coping with the void: firing a gun represents not only an assertion of "masculinity" for Clyde and an expression of hostility for Bonnie but also an extension of photography, an attempt to define both their selves. At the beginning of the film, Bonnie's mouth is shown half-opened with desire for something she cannot even name. But in our society, the first thing her lips come in contact with is Coca Cola—a drink which remains as American as Mom's apple pie, or as American as all those advertisements for Eskimo Pie, Burma Shave, Philip Morris, and the like, which disfigure the once Edenic landscape of the movie. Frustrated inhabitants of a society which makes responsible adulthood difficult to come by, and which denies satisfaction of basic human and spiritual desires, Bonnie and Clyde are doomed victims of arrested development.

After their first robbery together, Bonnie tries unsuccessfully to get Clyde to make love to her. "I might as well tell you right off," he says. "I ain't much of a lover boy . . . I never saw no percentage in it"; to which Bonnie replies: "Your advertising is just dandy. Folks'd just never guess you don't have a thing to sell." One of the immoralities of the average film is that

As Clyde (Warren Beatty) shows Bonnie (Faye Dunaway) his gun, he wiggles a matchstick in his mouth suggestively. Bonnie fondles the gun barrel with awe, and the viewer is left with no doubt on the score of symbolism. At the start of the film, sex and violence are linked.

it asks the viewer to identify with an individual who is both murderous and sexually potent. Such films scarcely ever suggest a causal relationship between sexual pathology and violent behavior. *Bonnie and Clyde* first presents its protagonist in an attractive, glamorous light; it is only later that the abnormal side of the hero emerges from behind the façade. Romantic sexuality, so Bonnie thinks, is a way out of ennui. And it is precisely this illusion which is ironically perpetuated by Clyde's impotence. Thanks to the mythology of our time, the viewer is led to believe with Bonnie that if only the couple could have intercourse all their other troubles would disappear. However, coitus performed in a satisfactory fashion, or carried to its orgasmic conclusion, is no magic solution to the problem of human existence (as the film makes clear before its brilliant and unforgettable conclusion).

Although Clyde is unable to offer Bonnie what she believes to be the ultimate experience in life, he does promise her what he conceives to be the highest reward in life: money. If Bonnie Parker is an Emma Bovary who exaggerates the importance of the romantic and sexual emotions, Clyde Barrow is a Willy Loman who has the wrong dream, who wants to come out the number-one man. It is another of the ironies in the film that the Barrow gang never makes much money. The diet of the gangsters seems to consist chiefly of hamburgers and Coca Cola. Like the common man in Arthur Miller's play, Bonnie and Clyde end up with nothing to show for their efforts.

The structure of *Bonnie and Clyde* is seriocomic and mainly horizontal. Throughout the film there is a fusion of laughter and grimness, the former more predominant in the first half, the latter in the second. In the beginning, when Clyde robs the first grocery store, the flight of the couple's car down the road is accompanied by Earl Scruggs and Lester Flatt playing "Foggie Mountain Breakdown" on the sound track. The twangy banjo accompaniment to the early chase scenes gives *Bonnie and Clyde* the quality of a Mack Sennett comedy; it underlines the satirical elements of the film; and most important, it hooks the viewer into the game the title characters seem to be playing—the game of movie violence, violence without pain or bloodshed. Structurally, the patterning in the film is not vertical, since none of the characters are examined in depth. From scene to scene, sequence to sequence, the emphasis is on action. Density in the film results from the complex rendering of theme through the interchanging of effects.

Following the sequence in which Clyde reveals his impotence and Bonnie decides to join with him anyway, there comes a scene that provides the couple with a rationalization for their life of crime. Bonnie and Clyde have slept the night in a deserted farmhouse. In the morning sun, Clyde teaches Bonnie how to shoot, showing the same patience and joy a father reveals in instructing his little daughter on how to ride a horse. A farmer appears and informs the couple that the bank has seized the farm from him. Full of sympathy, Clyde fires his gun into the foreclosure sign; the farmer and his black helper borrow the gun and also shatter the windows of the house. Before the farmer departs, Bonnie and Clyde introduce themselves, and Clyde adds with pride: "We rob banks." The farmer's eyes register skepticism—thus alerting the viewer to the couple's self-deception.

The serious scene with the farmer is followed by a comic one in which Clyde attempts to hold up a bank. After wearily informing the gunman that the bank went out of business three weeks back, the cashier is forced outside on the sidewalk where Bonnie is waiting in an automobile. Apparently, Clyde fears that Bonnie will have increased doubts about his "potency." The audience does not hear the brief explanation repeated by the clerk. Instead, Penn keeps his camera inside the bank and shoots the scene—which ends with Bonnie laughing at the ridiculousness of the situation—through the glass window. "We rob banks," Clyde had boasted to the farmer. But the bank here has nothing to rob. Again, Clyde fires his gun—this time shattering the window of the bank.

This mainly comic scene is followed by one which is serious and violent. Clyde robs another grocery store. But this time the huge butcher in the store attacks the hero with a meat cleaver. By keeping his camera in close to the action, Penn makes us feel Clyde's fear. For the first time in the film there is a suggestion that someone—including the hero—might be hurt. And before the scene is over Clyde shoots the butcher in the stomach and beats him on the head with his pistol. As their car speeds away, a terrified Clyde tells Bonnie: "Why'd he try to kill me? I didn't want to hurt him."

Next Bonnie and Clyde meet C. W. Moss (Michael J. Pollard), who works in a filling station. Bedazzled by the couple, the attendant joins up with them. Throughout the film, C. W.—a small, pixy-faced individual—looks upon Clyde as a superior being, a superman, one whom the police could never hope to outwit or bring down with bullets. Yet it is C. W. himself whose stupidity creates a situation in which Clyde kills a man for the first time, it is C. W. whose carelessness leads to a serious wounding of Clyde, and it is C. W. whose father helps set the police trap which results in the death of Bonnie and Clyde.

During the next bank robbery Clyde becomes wanted for murder. The scene begins in a comic fashion. C. W., instead of waiting for the couple outside the bank, parks the getaway car in a place down the street. When Bonnie and Clyde emerge from the bank, they look around wildly for the car but cannot find it. Down the street, C. W. tries unsuccessfully to wheel out of his tight parking space. Finally Bonnie and Clyde race down to the car, get inside, and urge C. W. to get moving. Again, it is a scene reminiscent of the Keystone Kops. But this time there is an abrupt change in mood. Just as C. W. swings the car free— the audience laughing uproariously—the bank teller appears and jumps on the running board. Frightened, Clyde shoots through the glass window of the car, hitting the teller point blank in the face.

Clyde Barrow is now a killer.

Cut to the inside of a movie theater. On the screen is a scene from the Busby Berkeley musical *Golddiggers of 1933*, the song "We're in the Money" played on the sound track. The camera picks out Clyde, Bonnie, and C. W. in the audience.

Bonnie and Clyde 1967

Bonnie remains thoroughly absorbed in the film-within-the-film, whereas Clyde is castigating C. W. for his lack of intelligence. "On account of you," Clyde says, "I killed a man." Annoyed by the disturbance, Bonnie twists in her seat. "If you boys want to talk, why don't you all go outside?" For Bonnie the world on the screen is more real than the one in which bank tellers are shot to death.

In a motel room Clyde suggests that Bonnie quit the gang, but she refuses to part from him. Deep down, Clyde is happy with her decision, even though he realizes the danger for both of them. Loyalty, and something close to real love, is beginning to develop in the relationship between Bonnie and Clyde. They kiss passionately. Suddenly Clyde seems hopeful; his expression suggests that their desire for each other can at last be consummated. After pulling down the shades, Clyde pads back to Bonnie who is lying on the bed. They embrace and kiss again. But it soon becomes obvious that this handsome, muscular male cannot even have an erection. Frustrated, Bonnie turns her head aside and, ironically, rests her cheek on the barrel of Clyde's gun. Once again, sexual gratification is denied to the lovers. And the illusion that eventually coitus will open the way to a thrilling new mode of existence in the future is sustained.

Clyde's impotency is merely symptomatic of a more fundamental problem, of a basic ineffectuality. In the scene following the one in the motel room, Clyde is joined by his brother Buck (Gene Hackman) and the latter's wife Blanche (Estelle Parsons). Although Clyde proceeds to bolster his ego by puffing on a cigar and showing off his gun—and in other ways acting suspiciously "masculine"—there is much more involved in the scene than an attempt to show how a sexually impotent man's defense mechanisms and sublimations function. For when the Barrow gang finish snapping each other's picture, when Clyde and Buck finish slapping each other's back and swapping corny jokes . . . there remain long moments of painful silence in which brother has nothing to say to brother. "We're gonna have ourselves a time, boy!" Buck shouts happily, clapping his hands. But then, quietly and sheepishly, he adds: "What're we gonna do?" Ours is a society, *Bonnie and Clyde* makes clear, in which true communication is difficult to achieve, in which men have no sense of community because they have nothing in common—nothing but alienation. Blanche is the daughter of a Baptist minister; C. W. Moss is a member of the Disciples of Christ. Institutional religion, set within the context of a commercial society, has failed to give meaning or direction to the lives of the characters in *Bonnie and Clyde*.

The first big gun battle in the film takes place in Joplin, Missouri. Clyde and the others are hiding out in an apartment on top of a garage. A delivery boy becomes suspicious of them and informs the police. As Bonnie reads aloud from a poem she has written entitled "The Ballad of Suicide Sal," Clyde looks out the window and suddenly cries: "The law's outside!" Immediately Blanche begins screaming—and her screams continue throughout the scene. Although the ensuing battle is extremely violent, the viewer is both numbed by the guns blasting, the rapid cutting, the bodies of policemen falling—and amused by the shrill unceasing sound of Blanche's voice. The chaotic scene ends on a deliberate comic note. As the gang escape by car, Buck asks: "Where's Blanche?" Shot of Blanche running down the residential street in what appears to be fast motion. At this point, the audience is nearly as hysterical as Blanche. In a long shot, Penn shows us the getaway car swerving alongside of Blanche and two hands reaching out and scooping her up and yanking her inside. Once more, a cinematic experience of unremitting violence is capped by a technique drawn from slapstick farce.

As a result of the gun battle at Joplin, the Barrow gang is now more famous than ever—and more wanted. We are never in any doubt about the outcome of the action: Bonnie and Clyde will die.

It is at this point that a Texas Ranger, Captain Frank Hamer (Denver Pyle), appears as a symbol of retribution, of the fate awaiting the couple. Parked in a wooded area near a lake, the gang read about themselves in a newspaper. Hamer sneaks up on them—but is himself captured by Clyde. Instead of killing him, Bonnie suggests that they take the Ranger's picture with them in it and send it to the newspapers as a way of humiliating him. However, when Bonnie kisses Hamer, he spits in her face and the comedy gives way to violence. Clyde goes berserk. Using a hand-held camera, Penn shoots Clyde and Hamer as they struggle and finally splash into the water. Again, instead of killing him, Clyde shoves Hamer into a rowboat and pushes him out on the lake. Bonnie shouts: "We're gonna put that picture in every paper in the country!" And Clyde yells: "We got you! We got you!" But Hamer does not answer. He merely stares across the water at them, implacably. Fade out.

Next the gang rob a small town bank. This is one of the most brilliantly edited scenes in the film, and most certainly one of the funniest. Crosscutting, though a staple of movies since the time of Griffith, is used here in a fresh and meaningful way. After the robbery, the gang drives off, pursued by two police cars. On the sound track we hear Flatt and Scruggs again. Penn cuts back and forth between the Barrow gang and the pursuing police, and between the chase and the interior of the bank. In order to show the audience how the average man—including the average guardian of the law—enjoys the excitement of crime, we listen to a bank guard declare how he stared "straight in the face of death"; and then—reacting immediately upon command—we watch him assume a striking pose for a newspaper photographer. This action economically links the picture-taking proclivities of the Barrow gang with the vanity of the average man. The chase scene ends with the Barrow gang crossing the border from Texas into Oklahoma. One of the policemen remarks: "I ain't gonna risk my life in Oklahoma." And the police turn back.

With about one-third running time left in the film, the mood grows increasingly somber, though almost right up to the end the humor never entirely disappears.

The gang kidnap a couple—Eugene Grizzard (Gene Wilder) and Velma Davis (Evans Evans)—and take them for a ride. At first the couple are frightened, but after awhile they relax and enjoy themselves. Buck pushes a gun in Eugene's face, says menacingly, "Now boy, when you gonna marry the girl?"—and then breaks into hearty laughter. Later everyone devours hamburgers in the car. When Bonnie learns that Eugene is an undertaker, however, her attitude changes at once. "Get them out of here," she snaps. What began as a pathetic attempt on the part of the gang to overcome loneliness, to become at one with others in love instead of being alienated by violence, concludes with the undertaker and his girl watching the Barrow gang drive down a dark road leading to death. Penn holds this shot on the screen for a long time—the image of the road looks forward to the ending of the film—before cutting to a scene of bright daylight as Clyde chases the runaway Bonnie through a wasteland-like field of dry corn. Bonnie wants her "Mama," and Clyde promises her that in spite of the dangers he will arrange a family reunion. Romantic music is then heard on the sound track . . . and it continues as a bridge into the next scene.

The family reunion—a picnic which takes place in a deserted sandy area—is shot in soft focus, resulting in a blurred or hazy effect. This technique, creating as it does an aura of unreality, remains appropriate for the scene. Similarly fitting is the discontinuity of the montage. Penn seems to give us a series of snapshots in monochrome; there is a bluish, dreamlike, truncated quality to the action, as movements begin but do not end. At one point, two boys roll down a hill in slow motion. During the whole of this idyllic expressionistic scene, one is reminded of the conclusion to Thomas Wolfe's *The Web and the Rock* (1939):

> ". . . and morning, morning in the thickets of the memory, and so many lives-and-deaths of life so long ago, together with the thought of Winter howling in the oak, so many sunlights that had come and gone since morning, morning, and all lost voices—'Son, where are you?'—of lost kinsmen in the mountains long ago . . . That was a good time then."
>
> "Yes," said Body. "But—you can't go home again."

Bonnie Parker—no less than Wolfe's George Webber—"can't go home again."

Bonnie and Clyde 1967

Two scenes of brutal realism—of almost unparalleled violence on the screen—follow the family reunion. The first scene involves a gun battle at the Platte City Motel. C. W. and Blanche go to a lunchroom and C. W. carelessly allows a deputy to see his gun. Later that night, as the gang listen to Eddie Cantor on the radio, the police attack. Buck is wounded in the head and Blanche is struck in the eye. Nevertheless Clyde and the others manage to escape to Dexter, Iowa, where another battle ensues. Here the Barrow gang is surrounded: Buck is killed (as he lies dying on the ground Penn shoots him from a high angle, a shot which foreshadows Clyde's death, for as the latter lies dead on the ground at the end Penn again uses a high angle set-up)*, Blanche captured, Bonnie and Clyde both seriously wounded—though once more they escape with the unharmed Moss. For a long time we have not heard the lighthearted playing of Flatt and Scruggs. But suddenly, as the trio make off, there it is again . . . only it is heard much more softly than before. This time Bonnie and Clyde are bleeding heavily, and no laughter issues from the audience. Crime and violence do not seem funny now.

C. W. takes his companions to his father's farm. At first, the elder Moss seems more concerned over the fact that his son has a tattoo on his chest than that he has been consorting with outlaws. Later, however, he plots to betray Bonnie and Clyde to Hamer in order to get C. W. a light sentence. Before he does so, Bonnie publishes a poem in the newspaper—a poem entitled "The Story of Bonnie and Clyde"—and Clyde is ecstatic. They are in an open field when she reads the poem to him. "You know what you done there?" Clyde says. "You told my story . . . You made me somebody they're gonna remember." The toothpick in Clyde's mouth is standing at attention. And at last, he and Bonnie are able to make love.

* Violence breeds violence. The law allows poor people to be violently removed from their homes and abused in countless ways. The Barrow gang is violent. But the agents of the law prove themselves just as violent, again and again. While Buck lies dying on the ground, the posse—who are whooping like wild Indians—surround him, hoping that he will succeed in reaching for his gun, so that they can pump more bullets into him.

161

But what has given Clyde his sexual potency? Apparently, the spurious ego-inflating conviction of immortality, the belief that the reality of the self, its genuine powers, has been liberated through Bonnie's trite poem. Although Bonnie and Clyde are sentimental, the film is not. Later in the picture, Bonnie asks Clyde what he would do if they had their lives to live over again. At first, Clyde is speechless. He makes a helpless, ineffectual gesture. Finally, he tells her that they would live in one state and rob banks in another! Is there any doubt that Clyde is still "impotent"? If the film were sentimental (as it has been accused of being), the hero would be seen conceiving of a better, more wholesome, life in the future. That Clyde cannot even imagine such an existence suggests the measure of his failure as a human being. Far from applauding him, the film shows how empty the man's life remains.

The scene depicting Bonnie and Clyde making love ends with a shot of the newspaper containing the poem blowing away into the woods. Something more than a cheap bit of verse, the film seems to be "saying," is required to invest man's existence with significance. Sex—no more than violence—cannot solve all the problems of life.

Cut to a shot of faded advertisements on a store front, followed by a slow pan in the opposite direction from that in which the newspaper blew across the ground. Here Penn has switched from a lens with a depth of field to a 400mm, or telephoto, lens with no depth. The impact is striking. Everything looks flat; the images appear to flicker and shake. Because it gives an abstract quality to what we see, the technique underlines the inhuman nature of what is to follow. Eventually the camera comes to rest on the exterior of Eva's Ice Cream Parlor. Inside are seated two men: one is the elder Moss, the other has his back to us. Penn keeps his camera outside. We see the lip movements of Moss, but we hear no words. The camera seems wary, as though it wanted to maintain its distance and not learn the language of betrayal. At length, Moss exits from the store; he glances about nervously—and the camera seems nervous too, as it appears to fidget in front of this Judas. A car

Bonnie and Clyde 1967

A shot of Bonnie and Clyde during the gun battle at Dexter, Iowa.
Bonnie and Clyde is a violent film with an anti-violence theme.

snaps past. Moss is gone. Then we see the other man—it is Hamer. The Texas Ranger wipes his mouth with a handkerchief, glances cooly left and right, and then he too disappears. Visually, the scene is unforgettable.

Few motion pictures have ended with the impact of *Bonnie and Clyde*. As the couple drive down a road in bright sunshine they see the elder Moss apparently having trouble with his truck. Here Penn uses a subjective camera. We are in the car—we see what Bonnie and Clyde see. Hence we are forced into an identification with the couple, and this identification will intensify our experience of the ending. The scene lasts two minutes on the screen; it took three days to shoot; two weeks to edit. But it is worth the pains taken by everyone involved. Clyde gets out of his car and moves across the ground to offer help to Moss. There is a shot of bushes behind which the police are concealed; suddenly birds fly out from nearby trees; and the sound of their wings prompts Moss to dive under his truck. All at once, Clyde knows that he and Bonnie have been caught in a trap. Close-ups of the lovers exchanging farewell glances—each knowing that this was the way they had both known it would end.

According to newspaper accounts, 120 bullets were fired by the police at the real Bonnie and Clyde, with about fifty hitting the pair. The film recreates this butchery. Penn had Beatty and Dunaway dabbed with waxen bullet marks. Each time one of them was supposed to be struck by a bullet, a technician, by remote control, exploded a tube of "blood" fastened to the actors' underwear. Penn also used four different cameras, each at a different speed, each with a different lens, to vary his effects. Clyde's death is recorded in slow motion, whereas Bonnie, who remains in the car, is pounded realistically by bullets. The juxtaposition of the two speeds here emphasizes a dual view of the outlaws—both the mythic and documentary aspects of their lives.

The final moments of the film, like its opening, are quiet. Hamer and the other policemen gaze at the bodies of the dead lovers—then, abruptly, the screen goes to black-and-white again, and the picture ends.

Bonnie and Clyde 1967

Click, and the story of Bonnie and Clyde begins; click and it is finished.

Bonnie and Clyde has been criticized for not telling the exact truth about the real Bonnie and Clyde; for romanticizing the pair by casting beautiful people in the title roles; and for not showing the police in as an attractive light as the outlaws. The film, however, was never intended to be a straight documentary account of a historical period. Although certain elements in the picture are historically correct, *Bonnie and Clyde* concerns itself more with legend than fact. The film is art, not life. As Aristotle pointed out, the historian focuses on the individual event, whereas the poet is interested in the universal—the necessary or probable principles which bind events together. Although *Bonnie and Clyde* might have been a better film if it had shown Hamer and the other representatives of the law more sympathetically, the argument over Warren Beatty and Faye Dunaway's good looks remains mere niggling criticism. The romanticism of *Bonnie and Clyde* is consistently undercut by the moral criticism which the film renders against the outlaws.

When the National Catholic Office for Motion Pictures gave *Bonnie and Clyde* an award as the best picture of 1967 for mature audiences, the organization was severely criticized by *America*, the national Jesuit weekly magazine. The majority of the Protestant nominating committee rejected *Bonnie and Clyde* because its "moral witness" was not clear. During the funeral for Senator Robert F. Kennedy on June 8, 1968, the national correspondent for C.B.S., Eric Sevareid, used the occasion to pontificate about *Bonnie and Clyde*. According to Sevareid, Penn's film obliged audiences to identify with two killers—the implication being that *Bonnie and Clyde* somehow contributed to the assassination of Senator Kennedy. Bosley Crowther reviewed the film no less than three times; unfortunately, the then New York *Times* critic was no more perceptive the third time around than he was on the first occasion. Crowther felt that *Bonnie and Clyde* glorified violence and lacked moral uplift. Hollis Alpert felt called upon to defend Crowther's judgment: "Where Crowther particularly irritates his colleagues, and a good many of his readers, is in his call for 'moral values' in films. This standpoint . . . is old-fashioned in critical circles. Only fuddy duddies like Tolstoy and other literary giants of the past would dare this kind of assertion.''[2]

Many people failed to grasp the real meaning of *Bonnie and Clyde*. Though art is involved with philosophy and morals—critics who deny this are only deceiving themselves, and attempting to deceive their readers—the "moral witness" of a great film is not delivered from a pulpit, nor is it true that the simpler a "message" is, the more wholesome it remains as art. Tolstoy was a great artist and a great man—but he was a poor critic. He considered *Uncle Tom's Cabin* great literature, but in *What Is Art?*, he omits from his list of great literary works all mention of the Greek tragedies and the plays of Shakespeare. Crowther and Alpert are right in insisting that films reflect a moral world; they err in that they fail to see the moral dimension that exists in *Bonnie and Clyde*. A sympathetic treatment of a criminal in a work of art is not necessarily at odds with a moral condemnation of his crimes. *Bonnie and Clyde* is a violent film with an anti-violence theme.

"The trouble with the violence in most films," Penn argues, "is that it is not violent enough. A war film that doesn't show the real horrors of war—bodies being torn apart and arms being shot off—really glorifies war." The director rightly denies that *Bonnie and Clyde* glorifies crime; he says: "it shows the squalor, the isolation, the terrible boredom of these people" (New York *Times*, April 14, 1968).

Bonnie and Clyde is not just about the thirties, and not just about modern American society; it is a revelation of the human animal in his spiritual hunger and resultant capacity for violence—a condition which would seem to represent the plight of most men living in the twentieth century.

Notes

Potemkin

[1] Sergei Eisenstein, "A Dialectic Approach to Film Form," in *Film Form and The Film Sense* (Cleveland: Meridian, 1957), p. 53, italics in original.

[2] Eisenstein, "The Cinematographic Principle and the Ideogram" (1929), in *Film Form and The Film Sense,* p. 30, italics in original.

[3] Eisenstein, "Film Language," in *Film Form and The Film Sense,* p. 111.

[4] Eisenstein, "A Dialectic Approach to Film Form," in *Film Form and The Film Sense,* p. 54.

[5] Both essays can be found in *Film Form and The Film Sense.*

[6] Eisenstein, "Methods of Montage," *Film Form and The Film Sense,* p. 74.

[7] Eisenstein, "Through Theater to Cinema," *Film Form and The Film Sense,* pp. 3, 5.

Citizen Kane

[1] Orson Welles, quoted in *Focus on Citizen Kane,* ed. Ronald Gottesman (Englewood Cliffs, N.J.: Prentice-Hall, 1971), p. 68.

[2] André Bazin, "The Originality of Welles as a Director," in *Focus on Citizen Kane,* p. 129.

The Bicycle Thief

[1] George A. Huaco, *The Sociology of Film Art* (New York: Basic Books, 1965), p. 17.

[2] Cesare Zavattini, "Some Ideas on the Cinema," in *Film: A Montage of Theories*, ed. Richard Dyer Mac Cann (New York: Dutton, 1966), pp. 216–228.

[3] Vittorio De Sica, in *Encountering Directors*, by Charles Thomas Samuels (New York: G. P. Putnam's Sons, 1972), p. 147.

[4] *Ibid*, p. 148.

[5] *Ibid*, p. 144.

[6] *Ibid*, p. 153.

[7] *Ibid*, p. 153.

Ikiru

[1] See Donald Richie's *The Films of Akira Kurosawa* (Berkeley: University of California, 1970), pp. 11 and 197–8. Richie quotes Kurosawa as saying that he has read the Russian novelists of the nineteenth century; indeed, in their work, he says he learned what it means to be an artist.

[2] Akira Kurosawa, quoted in *Interviews With Film Directors*, ed. Andrew Sarris (New York: Avon, 1967), p. 299.

La Strada

[1] John Russell Taylor, *Cinema Eye, Cinema Ear* (New York: Hill and Wang, 1964), p. 29.

[2] Federico Fellini, "My Favorite Film," in *Federico Fellini*, ed. Gilbert Salachas (New York: Crown, 1969), pp. 107–108.

[3] Fellini, "A Reconstituted Interview," in *Federico Fellini*, p. 115.

[4] Fyodor Dostoevsky, *The Brothers Karamazov* (New York: Macmillan, 1916), pp. 339 and 343.

[5] Fellini quoted in "The Long Interview," in *Juliet of the Spirits*, ed. Tullio Kezich (New York: Ballantine, 1966), p. 49.

[6] Fellini, "My Favorite Film," in *Federico Fellini*, p. 107.

[7] Fellini, "The Game of Truth," in *Federico Fellini*, p. 115.

On the Waterfront

[1] Elia Kazan, in *Kazan on Kazan*, by Michael Ciment (New York: Viking, 1974), p. 109.

[2] Stanley Kauffmann, *A World on Film* (New York: Delta, 1967), p. 48.

Notes

Wild Strawberries

[1] See *Bergman on Bergman*, ed. Stig Bjorkman, et al (New York: Simon and Schuster, 1973), pp. 131–133.

[2] *Bergman on Bergman*, p. 146.

[3] Andrew Sarris, *The American Cinema* (New York: Dutton, 1968), p. 235.

[4] *Bergman on Bergman*, p. 133.

[5] Jorn Donner, *The Films of Ingmar Bergman* (New York: Doner, 1972), p. 156.

[6] Bergman has admitted the influence of Strindberg's *A Dream Play*, See *Bergman on Bergman*, p. 138. For Strindberg's preface, see *A Treasury of the Theater*, ed. John Gassner (New York: Simon and Schuster, 1960), p. 111.

[7] *Bergman on Bergman*, p. 148.

[8] Ingmar Bergman, *Wild Strawberries* (New York: Simon and Schuster, 1960), p. 55.

[9] Ingmar Bergman, "Bergman Discusses Film-Making," in *Wild Strawberries*, p. 12.

[10] Ingmar Bergman, "Tribute to Victor Sjöström," in *Wild Strawberries*, p. 14.

The 400 Blows

[1] François Truffaut, "Who Is Antoine Doinel?", in *The Adventures of Antoine Doinel: Four Screenplays* (New York: Simon and Schuster, 1971), pp. 7–8.

[2] "Interview with François Truffaut," in *The New Wave*, ed. Peter Graham (New York: Doubleday, 1968), p. 93.

[3] Pauline Kael, *Going Steady* (New York: Bantam, 1971), p. 339.

[4] "Interview with François Truffaut," p. 89.

L'Avventura

[1] Antonioni quoted in "A Talk With Antonioni," *Saturday Review*, XLV (October 27, 1962), p. 27.

[2] Fellini quoted in *On the Set of Fellini Satyricon* by Eileen Hughes (New York: William Morrow, 1971), p. 16.

[3] Antonioni quoted in "A Talk with Michelangelo Antonioni on His Work," *L'Avventura* (New York: Grove Press, 1969), p. 231.

[4] F. Scott Fitzgerald, *Tender Is the Night* (New York: Scribner's, n.d.), pp. 276–277.

[5] *Tender Is the Night*, p. 201.

[6] Antonioni quoted in "A Talk with Michelangelo Antonioni on His Work," *L'Avventura* (New York: Grove Press, 1969), pp. 223–4.

Bonnie and Clyde

[1] Arthur Penn quoted in *The Director's Event*, eds. Eric Sherman and Martin Rubin (New York: Signet, 1972), p. 132.

[2] Hollis Alpert, "The Case of Crowther," *Saturday Review* L (September 23, 1967), p. 111.

Selected Bibliography

Alpert, Hollis. "The Case of Crowther," *Saturday Review*, L, September 23, 1967, p. 111.

Antonioni, Michelangelo. "A Talk With Antonioni." *Saturday Review*, XLV, October 27, 1962, p. 27.

———. "A Talk With Michelangelo Antonioni on His Work." *L'Avventura* (film script). New York: Grove Press, 1969.

Bergman, Ingmar. *Wild Strawberries* (film script). New York: Simon and Schuster, 1960.

Björkman, Stig, et al, ed. *Bergman on Bergman*. New York: Simon and Schuster, 1973.

Ciment, Michel. *Kazan on Kazan*. New York: Viking, 1974.

Donner, Jörn. *The Films of Ingmar Bergman*. New York: Dover, 1972.

Eisenstein, Sergei. *Film Form and The Film Sense*. Cleveland: Meridian, 1957.

Gottesman, Ronald, ed. *Focus on Citizen Kane*. Englewood Cliffs N.J.: Prentice-Hall, 1971.

Graham, Peter, ed. *The New Wave*. New York: Doubleday, 1968.

Huaco, George A. *The Sociology of Film Art*. New York: Basic Books, 1965.

Hughes, Eileen. *On the Set of Fellini Satyrican*. New York: William Morrow, 1971.

Kael, Pauline. *Going Steady*. New York: Bantam, 1971.

Kauffmann, Stanley. *A World on Film*. New York: Delta, 1967.

Kezich, Tullio, ed. "The Long Interview," In *Juliet of the Spirits*. New York: Ballantine, 1966.

Mac Cann, Richard Dyer, ed. *Film: A Montage of Theories*. New York: Dutton, 1966.

Richie, Donald. *The Films of Akira Kurosawa*. Berkeley: University of California, 1970.

Salachas, Gilbert, ed. *Federico Fellini*. New York: Crown, 1969.

Samuels, Charles Thomas. *Encountering Directors*. New York: G. P. Putnam's Sons, 1972.

Sarris, Andrew, ed. *Interviews With Film Directors*. New York: Avon, 1967.

———. *The American Cinema*. New York: Dutton, 1968.

Sherman, Eric and Martin Rubin, ed. *The Director's Event*. New York: Signet, 1972.

Taylor, John Russell. *Cinema Eye, Cinema Ear*. New York: Hill and Wang, 1964.

Truffaut, François. *The Adventures of Antoine Doinel: Four Screenplays*. New York: Simon and Schuster, 1971.

Selected Filmography

Antonioni, Michelangelo

Cronaca di un Amore (1950)
I Vinti (1952)
Le Amiche (1955)
Il Grido (1957)
L'Avventura (1959)
La Notte (1960)
L'Eclisse (1961)
Blow-Up (1966)
Zabriskie Point (1969)
The Passenger (1975)

Bergman, Ingmar

Monica (1952)
The Naked Night (1953)
Smiles of a Summer Night (1955)
The Seventh Seal (1956)
Wild Strawberries (1957)
The Magician (1958)
The Virgin Spring (1959)
Through a Glass Darkly (1960–61)
Winter Light (1961–62)
The Silence (1962)
Persona (1966)
Shame (1968)
Passion of Anna (1969)

> *Cries and Whispers* (1972)
> *Scenes From a Marriage* (1973)
> *The Magic Flute* (1975)
> *Face to Face* (1976)

De Sica, Vittorio

> *The Children Are Watching Us* (1942)
> *Shoeshine* (1946)
> *The Bicycle Thief* (1948)
> *Miracle in Milan* (1950)
> *Umberto D.* (1951)
> *Two Women* (1961)
> *The Condemned of Altona* (1962)
> *The Garden of the Finzi-Continis* (1971)
> *A Brief Vacation* (1975)

Eisenstein, Sergei

> *Strike* (1924)
> *Potemkin* (1925)
> *October* (1927)
> *The General Line* (1929)
> *Alexander Nevsky* (1938)
> *Ivan the Terrible, Parts I and II* (1941–1946)

Fellini, Federico

> *The White Sheik* (1952)
> *I Vitelloni* (1953)
> *La Strada* (1954)
> *Il Bidone* (1955)
> *Nights of Cabiria* (1956)
> *La Dolce Vita* (1959)
> *8½* (1962)
> *Juliet of the Spirits* (1965)
> *Fellini Satyricon* (1969)
> *The Clowns* (1970)
> *Fellini's Roma* (1972)
> *Amarcord* (1974)
> *Fellini's Casanova* (1977)

Selected Filmography

Kazan, Elia

A Tree Grows in Brooklyn (1945)
Sea of Grass (1947)
Boomerang! (1947)
Gentleman's Agreement (1948)
Pinky (1949)
Panic in the Streets (1950)
A Streetcar Named Desire (1951)
Viva Zapata! (1952)
Man on a Tightrope (1953)
On the Waterfront (1954)
East of Eden (1955)
Baby Doll (1956)
A Face in the Crowd (1957)
Wild River (1960)
Splendor in the Grass (1961)
America America (1963)
The Arrangement (1969)
The Visitors (1971)
The Last Tycoon (1976)

Kurosawa, Akira

Rashomon (1950)
Ikiru (1952)
Seven Samurai (1954)
The Throne of Blood (1957)
The Hidden Fortress (1958)
The Bad Sleep Well (1960)
Yojimbo (1961)
High and Low (1963)
Red Beard (1965)

Penn, Arthur

The Lefthanded Gun (1958)
The Miracle Worker (1962)
Mickey One (1964)
The Chase (1965)
Bonnie and Clyde (1967)

Alice's Restaurant (1969)
Little Big Man (1970)
Night Moves (1975)
Missouri Breaks (1976)

Truffaut, François

The 400 Blows (1959)
Shoot the Piano Player (1960)
Jules and Jim (1961)
The Soft Skin (1964)
Farenheit 451 (1966)
Stolen Kisses (1968)
The Bride Wore Black (1969)
The Siren of Mississippi (1969)
The Wild Child (1970)
Such a Gorgeous Kid Like Me (1972)
Two English Girls (1972)
Day for Night (1973)
The Story of Adele H. (1976)
Small Change (1976)
The Man Who Loved Women (1977)

Welles, Orson

Citizen Kane (1941)
The Magnificent Ambersons (1942)
The Stranger (1946)
Lady from Shanghai (1948)
Macbeth (1950)
Othello (1955)
Touch of Evil (1958)
Mr. Arkadin (1962)
The Trial (1963)
Falstaff (1967)
The Immortal Story (1968)
F for Fake (1975)

Distributors

The films discussed in this book are available from the distributors listed below. For information about rental fees, write to the distributor and ask for his latest catalog.

Cine-Craft Company
709 South West Ankeney
Portland, Oregon 97205

Janus Films
745 Fifth Avenue
New York, New York 10022

Macmillan Audio Brandon
34 MacQuesten Parkway South
Mount Vernon, New York 10550

Index

Index

Index